The Art of Picture Framing

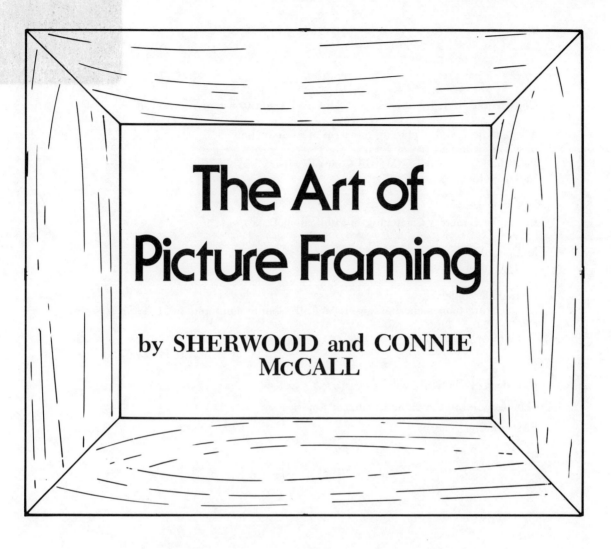

The Art of Picture Framing

by **SHERWOOD** and **CONNIE McCALL**

Illustrations by Gerald von Furstenberg
Photographs by T. Richard Young

THE BOBBS-MERRILL COMPANY, INC.
INDIANAPOLIS / NEW YORK

Copyright © 1981 by Sherwood P. McCall III and Constance A. McCall

All rights reserved, including the right of reproduction
in whole or in part in any form
Published by The Bobbs-Merrill Company, Inc.
Indianapolis   New York

Library of Congress Cataloging in Publication Data

McCall, Sherwood.
    The art of picture framing.

    Includes index.
    1. Picture frames and framing. I. McCall, Connie, joint author. II. Title.
N8550.M24   749'.7   80–2734
ISBN 0–672–52390–6

Designed by Bernard Schleifer

Manufactured in the United States of America

First printing

acknowledgments

THIS BOOK was a labor of love undertaken during the past few years as we continued to lead very busy lives. We could not have done it without the patience, encouragement and support of our families and close friends. We would like to say thank you to the many, many people who made this book possible.

To the late Evelyn Gendel, whose battle cry "Think Book" kept us going through many a long night; to our editor Lynne Spaulding who was ever so patient. Her enthusiasm was contagious.

To Houston Art and Frame and Jim Mulvey for the knowledge and background acquired in picture framing; to our neighbor and friend Ron Charlton who made it possible to keep two typewriters going at all times.

To Oris Robertson, Patricia A. Pike, Becky Kimes, John and Mary Jane Lippincott, Sam and Missie Lanham, Dr. James Helms, Michelle Braun, Patrick J. McCall and Don K. Langson for sharing their treasures with us and permitting us to photograph them.

To our families the McCalls and the Abells who were behind us every step of the way with ideas, encouragement and love; and last but not least to our five children, Jennifer and Mark McCall, and Cary, Scott and Todd Voelkel, who waited patiently "till the book was finished."

To our mothers
VIVIAN *and* KATHRYN
with love

CONTENTS

The Art of
Picture Framing

INTRODUCTION

EVERYONE HAS "FAVORITE THINGS," and long before I knew Sherwood a beautifully framed picture was on the top of my list. The walls of every room in my home were covered with a variety of framed items.

When Sherwood and I met he was horrified with the way many of my things were framed, and he slowly started reframing them. Although they had all been custom framed at various frame shops, I soon realized that I had missed one little thing here or there that kept them from being "just right." I was never intentionally misguided, but since I was not knowledgeable about the art of picture framing, I often ended up with the wrong thing, either in color, style, or technique.

Fortunately all that is changed now and our home is full of pictures we love. Since Sherwood and I have a "his and hers" family of five children ranging in age from eight to eighteen, we are never at a loss for material to develop new ideas. There is lots to frame around here!

The idea for this book started brewing when Sherwood sent me to the library to get a book on a special framing technique he was researching for a project he was doing. We realized there was a definite need for a book with good, creative ideas and basic framing techniques. Our purpose in this book is twofold. For those of you who want to do the entire procedure yourselves this book will lead you carefully and precisely through the steps from start to finish of a professional-looking custom frame job. For those whose time or interest does not allow that (it is time-consuming and often tedious work) we hope this book will serve as both a guide and idea book. There are so many different and unusual treatments that can be used on your pictures, and we hope to contribute our thoughts and ideas to help you in planning your frames. One idea leads to another, and you may develop many of your own designs from what we have to offer here.

For many of you this may become a hobby, and you will get great creative pleasure out of designing and executing the frames for family and friends. If you are a beginner you need to start with the simpler projects and then work up to the more difficult as you add tools and develop your skills. Framed items make wonderful gifts for graduation, wedding, new baby, new house—in fact, almost any occasion could be celebrated by the gift of a custom-framed picture.

Our hope is that you have as much pleasure and enjoyment from the art of picture framing as we do. Let your imagination take you beyond the ideas we give you and lead you into your own world of picture framing.

CONNIE McCALL

1

TOOLS

FOLLOWING ARE THE TOOLS you'll need in picture framing. The brands that we strongly recommend are mentioned. You can purchase most of these tools in either art supply stores or hardware stores.

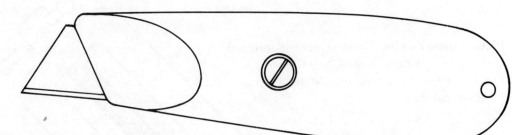

Utility knife. Used for cutting mats, mat board, cardboard, and backing board. Brand: Stanley.

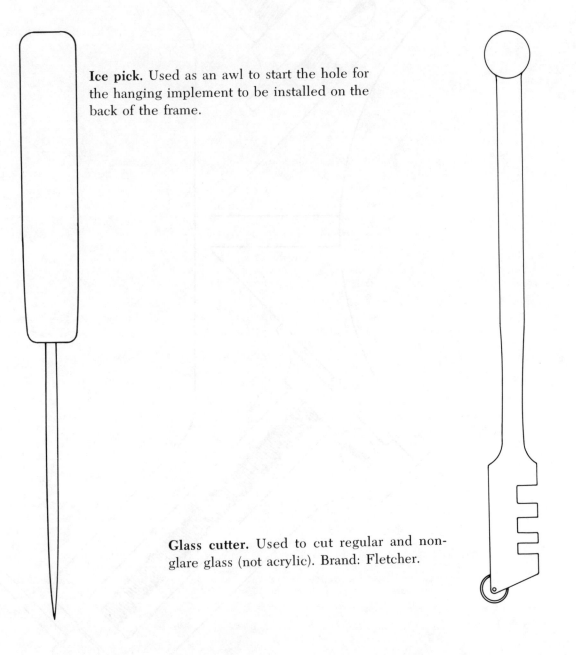

Ice pick. Used as an awl to start the hole for the hanging implement to be installed on the back of the frame.

Glass cutter. Used to cut regular and non-glare glass (not acrylic). Brand: Fletcher.

Picture framer's vise. Used to join the mitered corners of wooden frames together. Brand: Stanley #404 for home use, #400 for more professional use.

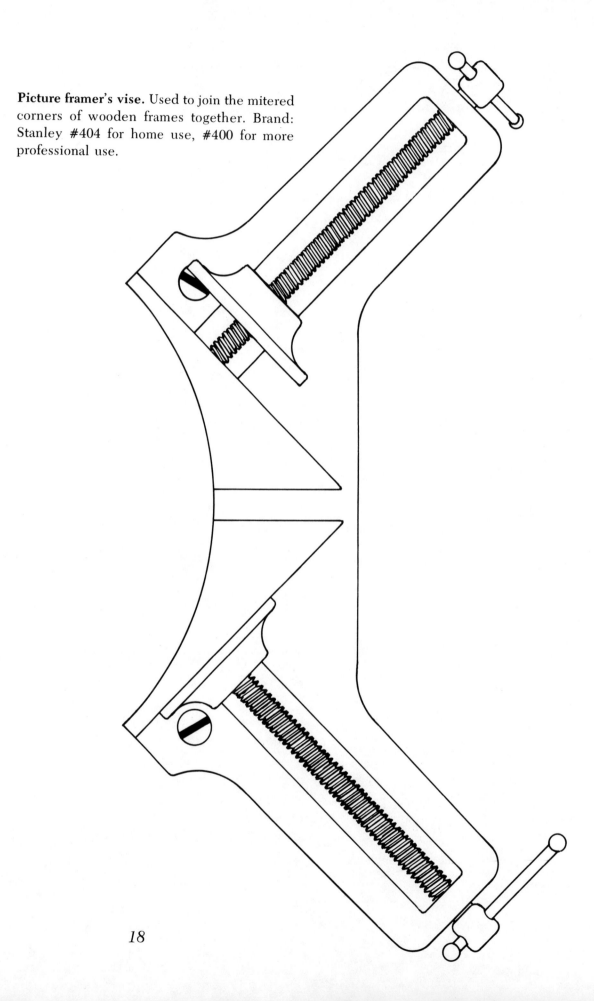

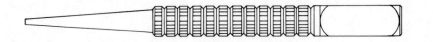

Nail set. Used to slightly set the nails into the wood of a frame so that a filler can be used that will match the frame. Brand: Stanley, size 1/32''.

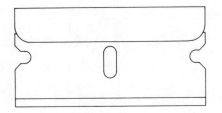

One-edge razor blade. Used to touch up the inner opening of a freshly cut mat. Also used to trim off dust cover from back of frame.

Emery board. Used to touch up the inside opening of a freshly-cut mat. Also used to trim off dust cover from back of frame.

Hammer. Brand: Stanley, 7 oz.

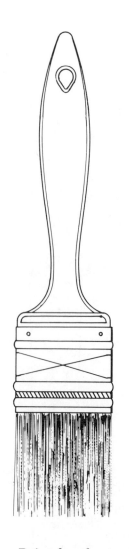

Paint brush. An inexpensive one of white bristles is fine. Used to sweep away dust from inside of frame and on pictures and mats before fitting.

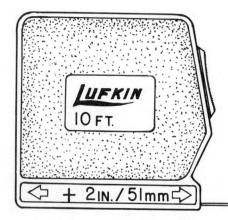

Measuring tape. Brands: Stanley or Lufkin.

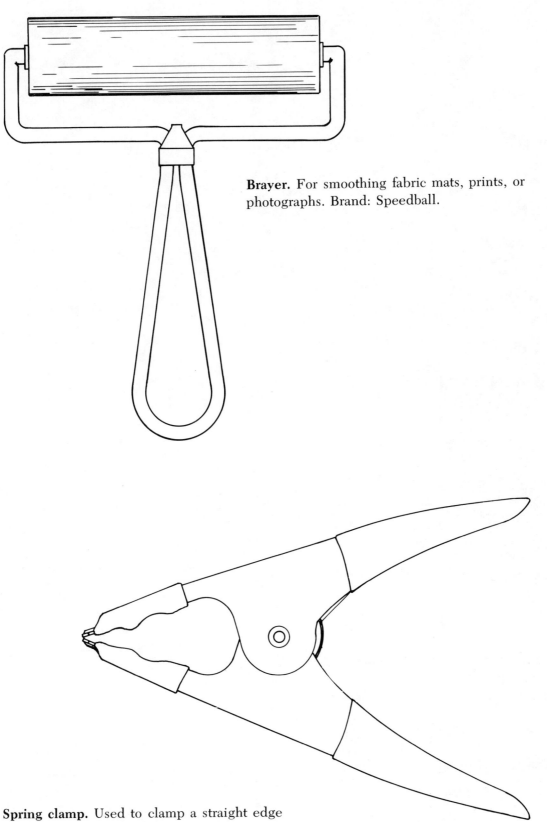

Brayer. For smoothing fabric mats, prints, or photographs. Brand: Speedball.

Spring clamp. Used to clamp a straight edge firmly in place over object you want to cut. Brand: Stanley #43-162P.

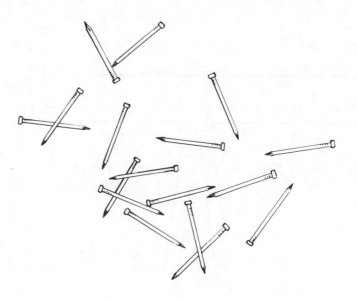

Brads. Used to hold a frame together or hold a picture in the frame. Brand: Tower wire brads.

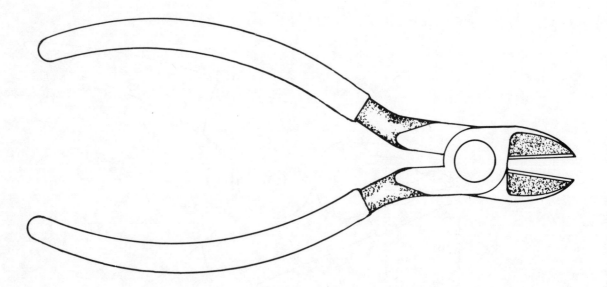

Wire cutters. Used to cut the wire for the back of the framed picture. Brands: Diamond or Klein. American-made wire cutters are far superior to foreign-made.

24″ metal ruler. Used to measure and as a straight edge for cutting the inside or outside dimensions of a mat. Brand: Stanley.

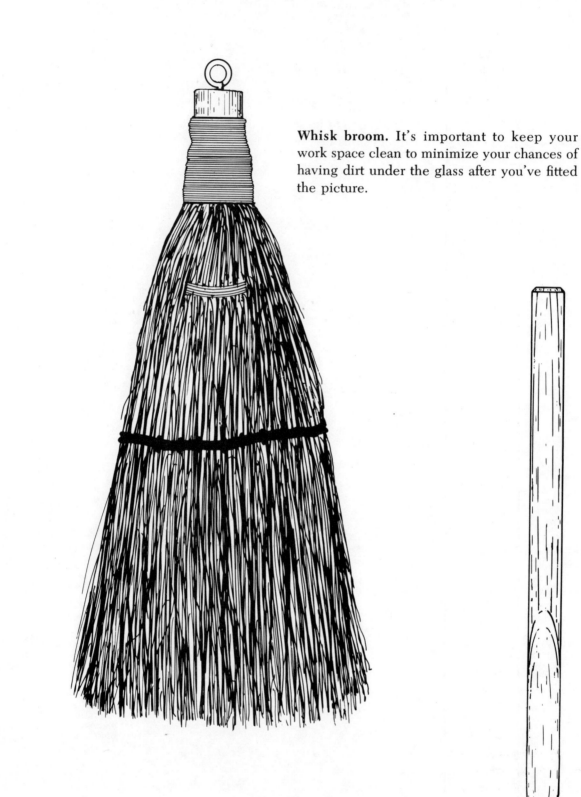

Whisk broom. It's important to keep your work space clean to minimize your chances of having dirt under the glass after you've fitted the picture.

Homemade putty stick. We have found that this design, made from a 3/8″ diameter wooden dowel, is ideal for filling cracks and nail holes in a frame.

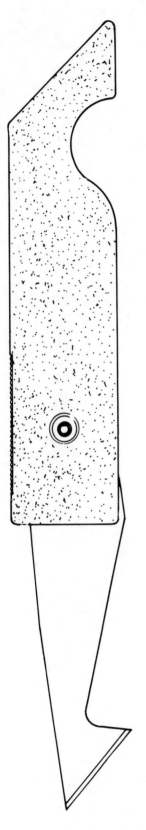

Acrylic cutter. Brand: Plastic Plus.

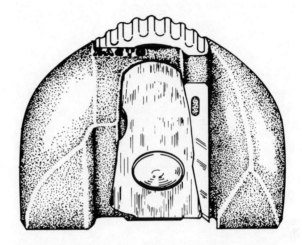

Beveled mat cutter. Used to cut the opening of a mat in beveled fashion. Brand: X-acto.

II
BASIC
INSTRUCTIONS

the mat

CUTTING THE MAT

TOOLS AND MATERIALS:
  mat board
  pencil
  ruler/straight edge
  spring clamp
  cutter (utility knife)
  cutting surface (noncorrugated cardboard)
  single-edge razor blade

OPTIONAL:
  X-acto bevel mat cutter
  T square
  X-acto No. 1 knife

OUTSIDE DIMENSIONS:

Decide the appropriate margin of mat you want around your picture. A Guide to Design on page 83 will help you with this.

You will now figure the total outside dimension in this way: Add double the width of the mat margin to each dimension of the picture. Thus, for an 8″ × 10″ picture with a 3-inch margin of mat, you must add 6″ (3″ on each side) to the width, making 14″; and 6″ to the height, making 16″. Your dimensions are now 14″ × 16″.

Now subtract ¼″ from both the height and width to allow the mat to cover ⅛″ all the way around the picture. (There will be exceptions on signed and numbered prints and lithographs. Check Chapter III, on design, for instructions on how to handle this.) Your dimensions will now be 13¾″ × 15¾″.

With a pencil and ruler you now mark off the outside dimensions on the mat board. We mark on the front of the mat board, as we prefer to look for the best part of the mat and check for any flaws.

Take the spring clamp and clamp your ruler, mat, and cutting surface to the table. We think the spring clamp is the key to cutting an accurate and precise mat, for it holds your ruler and mat snugly while you are concentrating on your nice clean cut. It costs around $3.00 and is well worth the money. With the spring clamp doing most of the work, you need only hold the top down with your hand to keep it from swiveling.

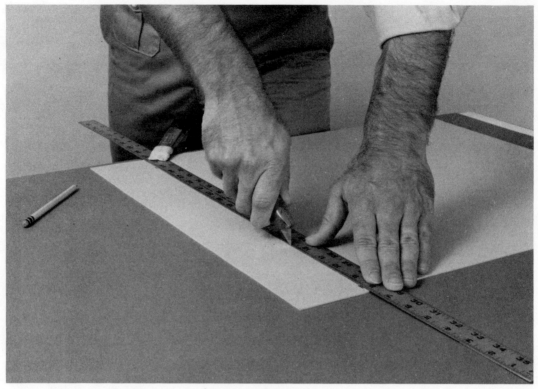
Cutting a straight-cut single mat

When you cut the mat, you should not cut through the entire thickness of it on the first stroke. With your utility knife, start by making a light score, concentrating on keeping your blade next to the straight edge. This score or groove will act as a guide for the cuts to follow. It will allow you to concentrate on applying more pressure while still cutting a straight line. Make at least two additional cuts.

Now reposition the mat to cut the next side in the same manner. It will be necessary to turn the mat each time you cut an additional side until all four sides are cut.

Now that you have cut the outside dimensions, you are ready to tackle the opening or the window of the mat. Following are instructions for both the beveled and the straight-cut mat.

CUTTING THE BEVELED MAT

For the beveled mat first mark your margins, then cut on the back side of the mat. For instance, if you have a 3″ margin planned, then with your ruler mark two dots 3″ in on each side of the mat, making a total of eight dots. Now place your ruler edge next to the two dots on one side and draw a line. Do this four times. The finished dots will look like a tic-tac-toe pattern.

Mat marked on back for a beveled cut

The beveled mat cutter is a push cutter: Your whole body weight is used to push the cutter across the mat. Before you begin to cut, set the blade so that when inserted into the mat the blade will barely protrude through the other side of the mat. If it protrudes too much it will drag into the cutting surface.

First, insert the blade into the mat at the bottom corner marks (left bottom corner marks if you are right-handed, and right bottom corner marks if you are left-handed). This is the most important part in cutting a beveled mat, as it will determine how well your corners come out. Take your time. Insert the blade into the mat, making sure the blade is parallel to the line, ⅛'' away from the opening—that is, on the margin side of the marks. This will prevent the pencil marks from being pushed into the bevel of the mat.

You may use either a T square or the ruler and spring clamp as your cutting guide, as long as the edge is stationary. A T square will work on mats up to 18''×24''; the spring clamp and ruler may be used on any size mat but are musts for larger mats. The T square base can be stabilized by holding the top part of the T square against the table with your hand. And, of course, the spring clamp will hold the ruler. Slowly move the straight edge next to the flat face of the mat cutter, being sure that the ruler is parallel with the pencil lines.

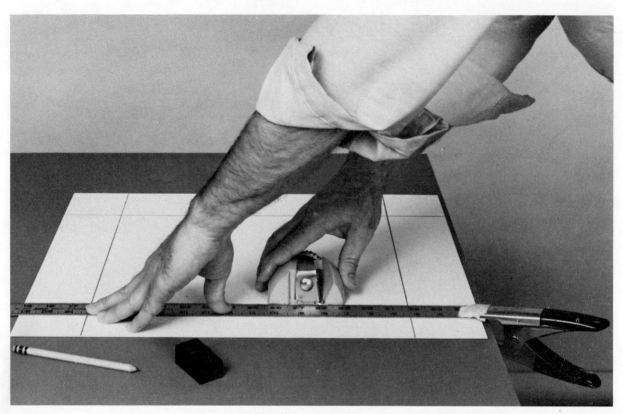

Cutting a beveled mat with an X-acto cutter

With your blade inserted into the mat, your T square or ruler and clamp firmly in place and parallel to the pencil line (about ¼'' off the pencil mark), you are now ready to push the cutter across the back of the mat. The design of the cutter is such that you need to put the straight edge ¼'' away from the blade to be ⅛'' away. With your other hand, hold the part of the ruler that isn't firmly anchored against the mat. Push the cutter away from your body with a downward pressure until the back of the blade is ⅛'' beyond the crossmarks.

Do all four sides like this, always remembering not to cut beyond ⅛'' of the crossmarks. Otherwise you stand a chance of overcutting on the front of the mat. It is always better to undercut your mat. If you have undercut you should now have a mat with the inner part still attached at all four corners by a strand of paper. Use a single-edge razor blade and insert it in the cut line near each edge to nip that final strand of paper. Now tip the mat and the center will fall out. If you have a rough edge use an emery board to sand it down.

A double-beveled mat is two mats on top of each other, with the inner openings of both mats beveled. To cut a double-beveled mat, take the mat that will be your inner mat and cut to the same outside dimensions as the first mat. Now take two-faced tape and stick a single strip all the way around the back of the first mat. Stick the two mats together, back to back. Now take a mat marker* that is the same width as you want to show on the inner mat and put the marker flush against the inner edge of the first mat. Mark all four inside corners of the second mat. Also make a corresponding mark on the side edge of each mat so that when you realign the bottom mat with the top mat you will have the marks to match them.

Pull the mats apart and make your cut exactly as you did on the first mat. Stick your mats together, this time being sure the back of the first mat is on top of the front side of the second mat. The two-faced tape should still be usable and should hold them together. You now have a beautifully cut double mat.

THE STRAIGHT-CUT MAT

We use a ruler to measure the corners of the mat and as a straight edge for our utility knife to follow; just be sure that your straight edge is as long as the longest side of your mat. We always use a metal ruler as our guide.

In the straight-cut mat you mark and cut on the front side of the mat. Due to the angle of the blade, you achieve a finer cut if you cut from the front. Take the ruler and mark the inside dimensions of the mat, making little pencil marks in each corner. Using a spring clamp, sandwich the mat between the ruler and your cutting surface. The window of the straight-cut mat is cut exactly the way the outside dimensions were, but you must be sure to put the point of the blade in at the crossmarks and stop cutting just before you reach the next set of crossmarks so you do not overcut them. If you can perfect these corners, your mats will always look professional. Remember, it is always better to undercut the corners because you can touch them up. When all your cuts are made you have a mat with the inside piece barely attached. Remove as you did in the bevel-cut mat. Be sure to erase any pencil marks.

For a double straight-cut mat, lay mat board for the inner window beneath the outer window, using two-faced tape between them. Fasten them both to the cutting surface and table with a spring clamp and mark the appropriate mat margins in each corner with a mat marker. Now use the ruler or straight edge held in place with the spring clamp, and cut the inner mat with a utility knife just as you did for the outer mat.

*You can make your mat markers from heavy cardboard or scrap mats. Make a series of markers about 1″ long and the desired width of your inner mat.

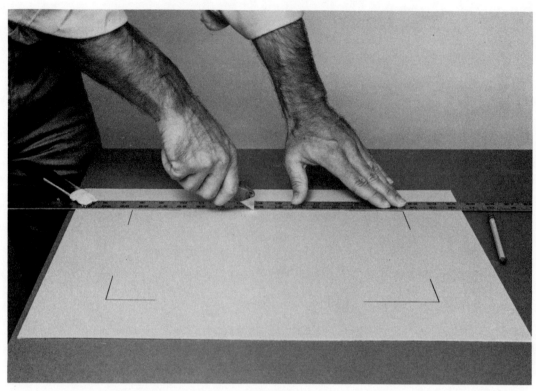

Cutting a straight-cut single mat

Cutting a straight-cut double mat

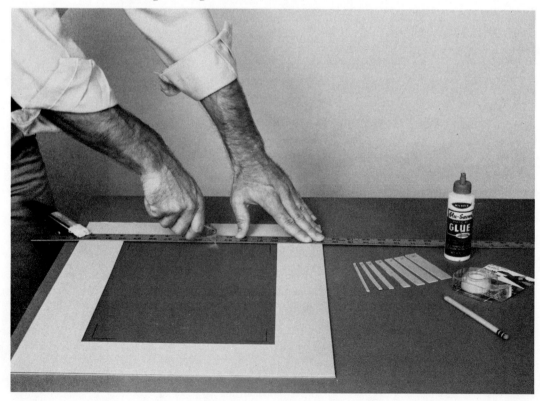

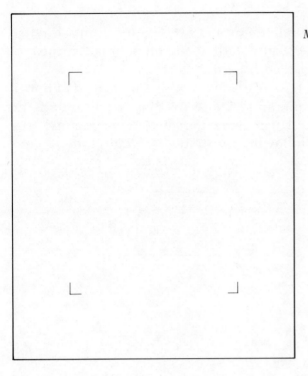

Mat marked on front for a straight cut.

VARIATIONS ON A MAT

ART DECO CORNER

Here we carry the Sculptured Corner (page 43) one step further and add a hole made from the back of the mat with an ice pick. Sand the rough edges with an emery board. This is very attractive if you use a double mat and the color from the inner mat shows through the hole.

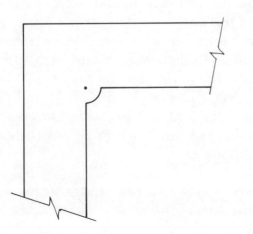

CHIPPENDALE CORNER

"Chippendale" relates to an eighteenth-century English furniture style. Its graceful outline and often ornate rococo ornamentation are characteristic of this style.

This type of corner works well with Colonial, traditional, and antique-type pictures. Do it by drawing lines off the straight-cut mat, and using the rounded-corner method (see page 42). Use the following illustration as your guide.

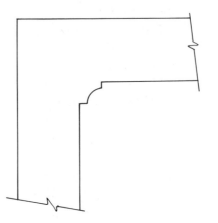

An antique Vanity Fair print from the "Spy series" called for special treatment. A double Chippendale mat was cut and a traditional moulding of antique gold with a black border was used to highlight the picture.

CIRCULAR MAT

Determine the outside dimensions and border that you want. As with an oval mat (see page 40), you will have a great deal more border visible, so where you might normally choose a 2″ rectangular mat you should cut the circle 1″ from the perimeter of the mat.

The drawing of a circular mat opening is much less complicated than an oval mat opening. Merely locate the center of the mat and place the point of a compass there. Place the pencil end of the compass at the border marks and draw the circle, then cut the circle as for the oval. You could also use the homemade compass described in the instructions for the oval mat. Cut and sand.

A circular mat lends itself well to baby pictures, snapshots, round objects such as coins and plates that you wish to frame, and, of course, round prints.

FRENCH MATTING

An extremely handsome technique, French matting is the placement of lines on the outer perimeter of the inside opening of the mat. You can use different colors and widths and sometimes more than one. The lines are usually painted on and it is an extremely difficult and time-consuming task. Here is a much easier method, and the same good-looking effect can be achieved. This technique can be used only on straight-sided mats—rectangular, square, etc.

In the art supply and architectural supply stores you will find a vast selection of pressure-sensitive graphic tape. It comes in different widths and different colors.

Draw a line around the inside opening of the mat with a pencil an appropriate distance from the inside edge—for example, ¼″, ⅜″, or ½″. Be certain to use a pencil for the line. Since the tape is pressure-sensitive you merely pull it out of its container and place it on the pencil lines. As you reach the corners, overlap the tape and then miter the corners with a single-edge razor blade or an X-acto No. 1 knife. Pull off the excess. Another line may be added a small distance from this and a line could go ¼″ away from the outside lip of the frame. All sorts of combinations can be used. Let your imagination go wild. This method is much easier than the traditional way of drawing or painting the lines on.

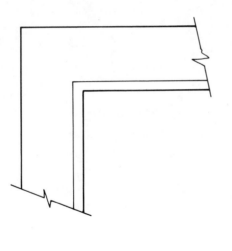

A great look without a great expenditure! An old frame was the starting point and the mat was cut to fit it. The French line was made with 1/32″ archural tape.

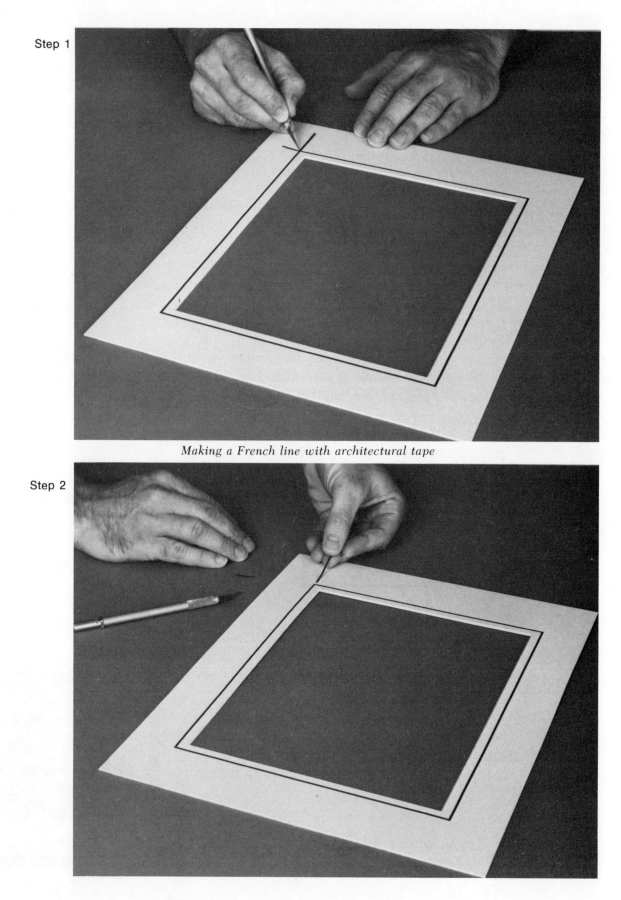

Step 1

Making a French line with architectural tape

Step 2

38

HEART-SHAPED MAT

Draw half a heart on a piece of paper (one that will fit the composition of the lovers' picture), fold it in half, and cut the heart out. This will give you an evenly shaped heart on both sides. Lay it over the picture and if it does not fit properly, merely trim or redraw if necessary.

Determine the outside dimensions of the mat before drawing the heart shape on the mat. Center the heart pattern on the mat and draw the heart shape on the top side of the mat.

Now you are ready to cut. The utility knife will work well with this shape. Make the first cut light and concentrate on following the shape of the heart. Make all the following cuts heavier, for the first groove in the mat will act as a guide for the following cuts. After cutting out the heart, sand with sandpaper or an emery board.

You have the option of covering this mat. To make it especially puffy, ours was stuffed with rubber foam and then covered with velvet. It's bursting with love!

OVAL MAT

As you determine the outside dimensions of your oval mat, remember that more mat will be visible than in a rectangular or square mat. To compensate for this you should choose a smaller border. For example, if you would normally have a 2″ border on a rectangular mat, a 1″ border would be ample for the oval mat.

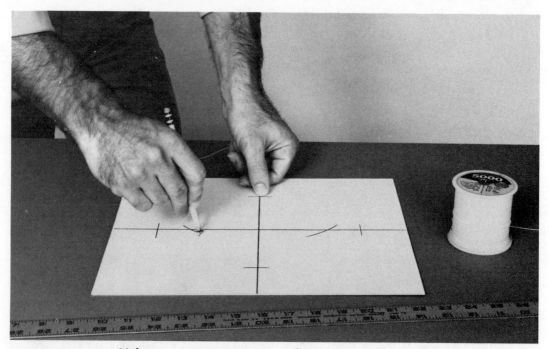

Making a compass to measure the oval mat

Drawing the oval mat

40

On the back of the mat draw horizontal and vertical lines intersecting at the center back of the mat. Always do this in pencil, preferably a No. 2 or a No. 3. If you have chosen a border of 1″, then measure in 1″ on the back of the mat and make a crossmark at the vertical and horizontal lines 1″ in from the outside dimension of the mat. These will give you the length and width of the oval.

To draw the oval you need to find the two focus points, A and B, on the longer line. Place the point of your compass at the exact center of the mat where the lines intersect. With the compass stationary, move the pencil end to the 1″ border mark of the longer line. With the compass set at this measurement, place the point of the compass at the point C mark on the shorter line, being careful not to move the setting of the compass. With the point of the compass stationary, draw an arc at either end of the longer line. This will create points A and B.

If you are cutting a larger oval mat you will have to make your own compass. Simply take a piece of nylon wire or fishing line (something that will not stretch) and tie one end around a pencil. Where you would normally put the point of the compass you will put the other end of the wire, hold it down with your thumb, and mark A and B.

Now place a brad at the two focus points (A and B) and *one* tack at *one* of the border marks (point C). Choose either end; it doesn't matter. Again, take a string that will not stretch and tie it tightly around the three tacks. It must be snug, for when you are drawing the oval you will have slight tension. Pull out the

Mat marked for cutting oval. Note: brad at point C is pulled out before oval is drawn.

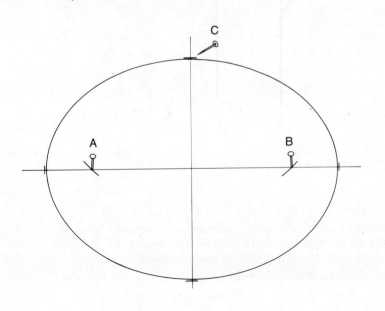

tack that is at point C. Put the pencil inside the string, then through a screw eye or button to keep the string from sliding off the pencil, and trace the pencil around the inside edge of the string, and you will draw an oval.

Using a utility knife, place the point on the oval and make a groove in the mat all the way around. Be sure that the groove does not go all the way through the mat, so you can concentrate on making the oval. The groove will act as a guideline for all the remaining cuts. Sand the edges.

To achieve a custom look you should cover the oval mat with fabric. Follow directions for covering a mat with fabric, page 44. This method will hide any flaws you may have in the cut. In both the oval and circular you make the slits in the fabric to ½'' apart all the way around the opening before gluing the fabric down. The closer the slits are to one another the better the fabric will conform to the curve of the oval or circle.

ROUNDED CORNERS

Do not feel you must use a straight-cut mat on everything. If the art piece has rounded lines to it then a rounded-corner mat is very much in order. Follow the instructions for cutting a

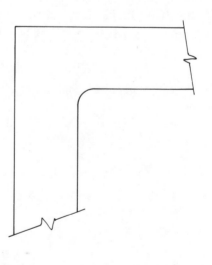

A nickel and a dime were used to cut the rounded-corner mats for this antique bird print. A moulding in silver-leaf with a similar contour to the bird was chosen to carry through the lines of the mat, frame and bird.

42

straight-cut mat, stopping about ¼'' away from the corner. If you want a big arch you will need to leave more space. Then place a nickel, a penny, or a dime on the inside of that corner and with a pencil draw the rounded line.

Using a utility knife, spring clamp, and straight edge, make the straight cuts on the front side of the mat, being sure to stop before you reach the rounded corner. If you are experienced with a utility knife, then you can use it to cut the rounded corner. An X-acto knife No. 1 has a thinner blade and will make the curve easier to cut. After cutting, sand with an emery board. If you want a double mat, then you must measure the inner mat with a coin or rounded object smaller in circumference than that used for the outer mat. A combination that works well is a nickel for the outer mat and a dime for the inner mat.

SCULPTURED CORNER

This effect can be achieved by reversing the rounded corners and making the rounded part go inward. You use the same techniques and objects that are used in the rounded corner mats. The effect is unusual and would work well with the more traditional and antique-type pictures.

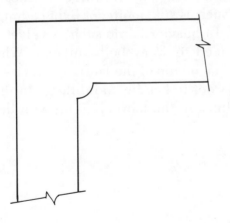

COVERING A MAT

MATERIALS NEEDED:
    paper mat already cut
    heavy-duty wallpaper adhesive or spray glue
    paintbrush (be sure it is one that doesn't shed)
    fabric (cut at least 1″ larger than the outside dimensions of the
        mat)
    utility knife
    spring clamp and metal ruler

SPRAY GLUE METHOD

First, find a room with good ventilation. Cover a large enough area with newspaper to catch the overspray. Never spray and frame in the same room. **It is very important to avoid breathing the spray.** The drying time is only a minute or two, hardly enough time for the air to clear if you spray and frame in the same room. We use the bathroom in our house with an exhaust fan (the smell tends to linger) and use an oversize closet for the framing.

Any color mat can be used as long as the color will not show through. If the fabric is light (such as silk), you will need to use a light-colored mat. If the fabric is an open weave, such as burlap, you should use a similar shade.

Cover your fabric with spray on the back side. Now spray your cut-out mat on the right side. Leave them until the glue is *very* gummy and sticky—about three minutes. If it is a very light material such as silk, moire, or light cotton, you need only spray the mat. In heavier fabric such as velvet, suede, or burlap you will need to spray both surfaces. When the glue is ready, lay the mat on top of the fabric—not vice versa, because the fabric is harder to handle and difficult to line up. Also, be sure that the lines in the fabric line up with the outside edge of the mat.

This well-known Albrecht Durer print of the hare is enhanced with a linen-covered mat and a traditional frame.

Viewed from the back, this shows fabric attached to paper mat.

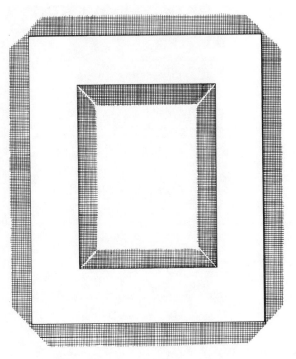

Fabric trimmed before folding.

Fabric folded to back of mat.

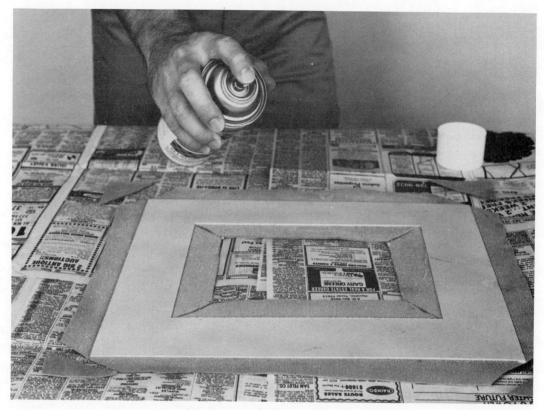

Spray-gluing the back of fabric and the mat

Rub your hand across the back of the mat, pressing the mat against the fabric. Wait a couple of minutes until the exposed glue on the excess fabric is dry.

Now turn the mat face up and with clean hands be sure that the fabric is pressed firmly down all around the mat. If there are any bubbles and wrinkles and you can't get them out, take an iron (on low heat), place a piece of fabric or paper (not newspaper) over them, and iron the fabric flat. This shouldn't be necessary very often. We are now ready to cut the fabric on the inside window of the mat.

Cut out an opening in the fabric, leaving at least 1″ of excess fabric to wrap around the back of the mat. Now cut diagonal slits from each inside corner, being sure that the slit goes all the way to the inside corner of the paper mat. At the four corners of the inside opening, put a small dot of white glue. This will keep the corners from fraying where the fabric is wrapped around the mat.

Again lay out papers in another room and spray glue the back of the mat and the fabric hanging loosely off the paper mat. Wait until the glue is very tacky and wrap the excess fabric around the back of the mat. Wrap the inside excess first and then the outside excess. If the two pieces of excess fabric happen to overlap (as they well might in a narrow mat) you can trim the edges so you won't have lumps. This would cause the mat to lay unevenly on the glass. Your fabric-covered mat is now complete.

WALLPAPER ADHESIVE METHOD

The wallpaper adhesive method is more troublesome than the spray glue method and it takes longer to dry, but it has some definite advantages. If you have limited working space and if you don't have proper ventilation, then this is the best method for you to use.

Again, you can use any color mat if the fabric is heavy, but if it is light, such as silk, you will need to use a mat board that is about the same color as the fabric. Also, an open-weave fabric like burlap calls for a corresponding color mat, as some might show through. Cut your paper mat and your fabric to the necessary dimensions. You can cut the fabric with scissors or a utility knife; the fabric will be 1" larger than the mat on all four sides.

In the gluing process we use Adhesium, a heavy-duty vinyl paste, but we're sure that any heavy-duty wallpaper adhesive would work. Brush the adhesive on the front of the mat using a 1"-wide brush. You don't have to glue both surfaces. The adhesive is thick enough that one surface will be sufficient, whereas gluing both surfaces could cause the fabric to stain. After brushing the front of the mat with glue you are ready to lay the mat on the fabric. Be sure that the fabric is face down on the working table. Lay the mat on the fabric (*not* the fabric on the mat).

Turn the mat right side up so that the fabric shows. Press the fabric down with clean hands. Lay a piece of scrap mat, glass, a board, or any hard, flat surface over the fabric-covered mat and add a weight of some sort. About 2 lbs. evenly distributed will be fine. Let it dry for about an hour. Remove the weight.

Cut an inside opening in the fabric in the center of the mat. Cut diagonal slits from each inside corner, going all the way to the inside corner of the paper mat. Now brush glue on the excess fabric, which will be wrapped around the back of the mat. You want the excess fabric from the outside edge of the mat to meet the excess fabric from the inside edge of the mat. If they overlap, you should trim the excess, or you will cause a ridge on the back of the mat. A ridge will make the mat lay unevenly on the picture or the glass when you fit it up. Again put weights on the mat and wait about two hours until dry. Your mat is now finished.

the glass

CHOOSING THE GLASS

The most commonly used glass is regular glass. It is very shiny and produces glare when light hits it at certain angles. The advantage of regular glass is that there is no distortion no matter how far back the picture is set into the frame. For instance, a shadow box needs regular glass. The cost of regular glass is much less than nonglare glass or acrylic.

A popular glass is nonglare glass, because it cuts out the glare from both natural and artificial light. We do not recommend it, however, if you are planning to use more than one mat on the inside of the glass. The farther the nonglare glass is from the picture the more distortion you will have. However, if you do want to use this glass with fabric or double mats, you can get around the problem by having them on the outside of the glass.

Acrylic has some advantages over both regular glass and nonglare glass. If you are framing a huge picture, acrylic would be a lot lighter. It is also good when the object must be shipped, since acrylic does not shatter. Acrylic is really better than regular glass for fine art on paper. Acrylic allows fine watercolors and drawings with subtle lines to be appreciated without discoloration, as regular glass has a slight greenish tint. But do take care, since acrylic scratches. You can buy it with an ultraviolet filter in it to protect valuable artwork from sunlight and artificial light.

CUTTING GLASS AND ACRYLIC

It's easiest to take your frame or dimensions to a retail glass company and have them cut the glass to fit your frame. This will guarantee a true fit. However, this service may not be available to you, and since you may be interested in learning to cut glass anyway, we will make our guidelines as simple as possible.

TOOLS AND MATERIALS:
glass
felt-tip pen
masking tape
ruler
spring clamp
glass cutter (metal- or carbide-tipped)

Regular and nonglare glass come in standard sizes:

8″×10″	18″×24″
9″×12″	20″×24″
11″×14″	24″×30″
12″×16″	24″×36″
14″×18″	30″×40″
16″×20″	36″×48″

If your frame has an inside dimension of 15½″×19¾″, then cut the dimension from a piece of glass 16″×20″. If you have it cut at a glass company, they will charge you for the full sheet of glass. Acrylic comes in very large sizes—4′×6′ or 4′×8′. In this case, they usually charge by the square foot.

First, lay the glass on the table. Measure the width of the glass along one dimension, and mark it by placing a dot at both of these edges. Be sure the remaining dimension is long enough for the length. You can either cut the glass free-hand by making a straight line with your felt-tip pen all the way across the glass where you plan to cut, or with a ruler and spring clamp. If you are a beginner, the ruler and clamp would be best. If you use a metal ruler, stick some masking tape on its underside so it doesn't scratch the glass. Place the tip of the cutter on the dot farthest from you and lay the ruler on the glass so the ruler touches the edge of the cutter. Spring clamp the ruler down on one end, holding the other end down with your hand.

Now pull the cutter toward you, putting enough pressure on the glass to score it. Pull the cutter all the way to the other end of the dimension. Now it is ready to break.

Remove the clamp and bring the glass toward you with the score perpendicular to the table, and the glass barely hanging off the table. With your two thumbs on the top of the glass (one on either side of the score) and the rest of your hands on the underside of the glass, break the glass downward and it will break all the way across the glass on the line you have made with the cutter. If the perimeter of the glass is 72″ or larger, hang the glass off the edge of the table with the score parallel to the table and touching the edge of the table. Using both hands, grasp the glass, and break downward. Be sure to support the hangover with your hands until the glass is separated.

Scoring the glass

Breaking the glass

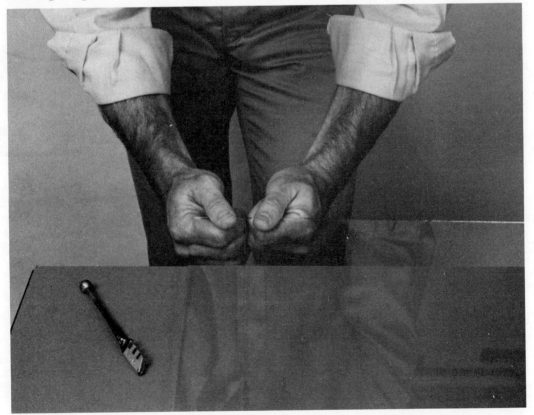

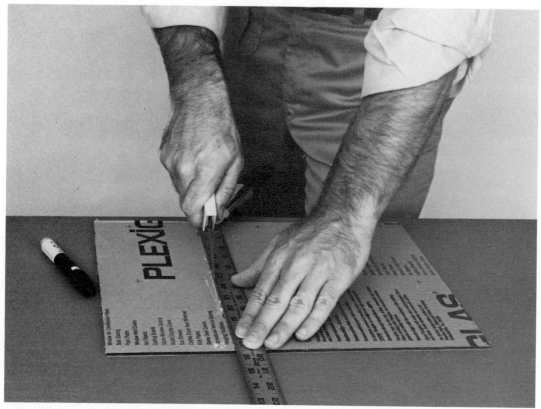

Cutting acrylic

Breaking acrylic

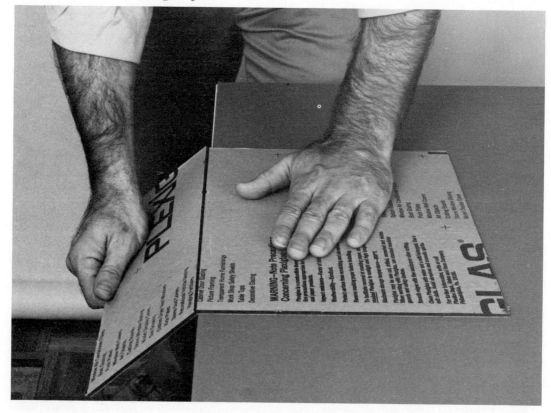

Do the same for the length.

Warning: Be careful when handling the glass, because the edges are very sharp. Always handle the glass vertically until you lay it down on the table.

Measure acrylic or plastic much the same way as the glass. The acrylic comes covered on both sides with a layer of thin, rubbery, plastic-coated paper. Do not remove this until the acrylic is cut and ready to fit in the frame. It will keep the acrylic from getting scratched. Remember again to make the dimensions approximately ⅛″ less than the inside dimension of the frame. It may be easier for you to measure the outside dimensions of the picture or mat that will fit into the frame. When you mark your dimensions be sure to mark them on the protective covering.

Mark your dimensions and line up your ruler on the marks you have made. Figure it out so you will have the most amount of scrap left over to use for other projects.

Clamp the ruler and acrylic to the cutting surface and table. This is not a push cutter but a pull cutter, so place the point of the cutter at the farthest part of the line and pull toward you. Start slowly to make a light groove all the way across the plastic. Make the following cuts stronger and deeper. The noise will be very squeaky. After making five or six cuts on the plastic, remove the metal ruler and clamp and line up the groove in the acrylic with the edge of the table. Push down on the groove and the piece of acrylic should break right off. Cut your other dimension the same way.

Acrylic is available ¹⁄₁₆″ thick in sizes up to 12″×16″, and ⅛″ thick in sizes up to 4′×8′. The main advantages are the light weight (this would come in handy in very large pieces) and the fact that it does not shatter. You can use it if a picture must be shipped, and it also makes a picture childproof. In addition, it gives a clearer viewing quality than glass. However, acrylic scratches easily and is harder to clean than glass. In the chapter on conservation mounting you can read about the special acrylic with an ultraviolet filter to protect valuable artwork from sun and fluorescent lights.

cutting and joining the frame

You have a couple of alternatives in cutting your frame. One is to go to a custom-framing shop, choose a moulding, and have them cut it for you to your specifications. They will have a large selection of mouldings, and you will still save a lot of money by doing the rest of the labor yourself. You can also buy moulding in stick form at a discount hardware store or lumber yard, and saw it yourself, as explained below.

CUTTING THE MOULDING

TOOLS
    miter box
    ruler or tape measure
    spring clamp or C clamp
    fine-tooth saw
    moulding
    pencil

First, figure the correct dimensions of your frame. To do this, add $1/16''$ to both dimensions of your picture. For example,

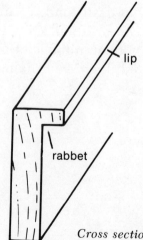

Cross section of a piece of moulding.

a 16″×20″ picture takes a 16 1/16″×20 1/16″ frame. You need the added 1/16″ to allow for any movement in the picture caused by climate.

On the inside of the moulding a rabbet—or recess—has been cut, into which the glass and picture will fit. It is along the rabbet that you will measure the dimensions of the frame. With the rabbet facing up, and the lip edge of the moulding away from you, mark off your first dimension from the right end of the moulding.

If the end of the moulding is not mitered (that is, cut at a 45° angle so that the corners can be joined), then you must do it. Place the moulding, again with the bottom against one side of the box, with the right end in the box.

There are a number of grooves diagonally along the length of the box. In making the first cut you will place the fine-tooth saw into the right groove that is cut out in the miter box. This

Sawing a frame using a miter box

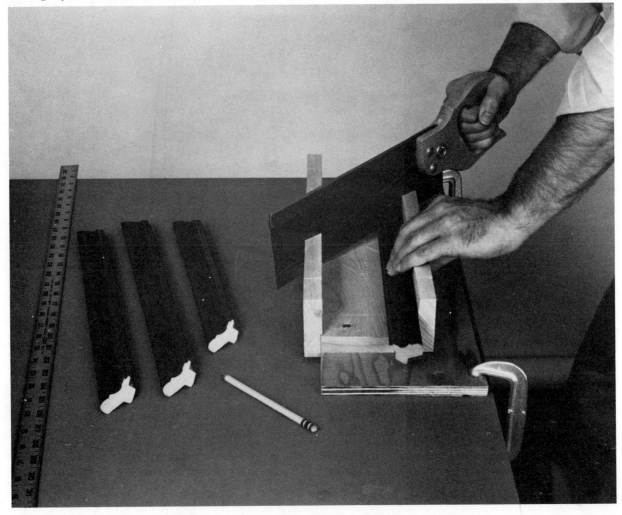

right groove will cause the saw to angle across the miter box to the appropriate groove on the opposite side of the box. Position the moulding so that the least amount of it is cut from the end, as you don't want to waste any wood.

In making your cuts you want to be sure to start off very slowly, exerting very little pressure, and then more pressure as the cuts get deeper. These first cuts will give you more control, thus allowing you to exert more pressure.

After you have cut the first miter, you are ready to cut the other end. This time, with the lip of the moulding still away from you, place your saw in the left groove and saw your miter in the opposite direction—but first reposition the moulding so that this cut will pass through your pencil mark. Now cut this end.

Now you are ready to cut a second length from your stick of moulding. The end of the moulding will have the wrong angle, resulting from the last cut, so you should cut this odd piece off to begin again with a proper angle. When you cut the second piece of moulding, cut the two pieces that will make the length. You want to be sure it is the exact size of the first piece. You can put the first piece on top of the moulding and mark it to be sure you get the identical size.

Now measure and cut your third and fourth sides in the same manner as you did the first two.

JOINING THE FRAME

TOOLS AND MATERIALS:
  small vise (screwed to a piece of board that can be clamped to a
    table)
  brads or finishing nails (as long as the moulding is wide)
  glue (white) or an aliphatic resin glue (yellow)
  hammer

OPTIONAL:
  drill
  nail set

Lay the long pieces of the moulding together to one side of the vise, and the short pieces on the other side (so you do not join the long pieces together when they should be on opposite sides of each other).

Place a long section in the vise and close the vise, gripping the moulding snugly. Now place a short piece in the vise and move the two mouldings together until the mitered corners meet perfectly. Now adjust your vise grips, first adjusting one and then tightening the same one. Then adjust and tighten the other side. Keep doing this until both corners meet perfectly. You want to be sure your corners are flush against one another all along the mitered edge. If you have done all this and they are still uneven, then there may be a little snip of wood on the inside. This can be sanded off easily.

Make sure that the edges of the corners are not overlapping. Sometimes there will be a slight difference in the width of the moulding. Make any adjustment on the inside. Nip off, sand, or hammer it down with the frame in the vise. You will probably need to touch up the frame with stain, paint, or a felt-tip pen. This can be done on each corner while it is in the vise. If you are working with unfinished wood, whatever finish you put on later will probably take care of any touchup needed.

Now you are ready to glue and nail. Remove one stick from the vise and put some glue on the raw edge. (For a really good bond, brush the mitered edges with a mixture of half water and half glue and let dry several minutes prior to final gluing.) Put glue on both miters, but don't put on so much that it runs out on the top and bottom. Wipe off what does come out. Place the

Nailing a frame together

Setting a nail

*Filling in nail holes
with crayon wax*

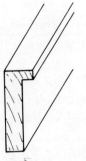
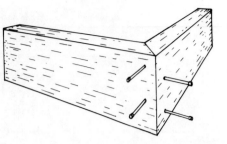

*Cross sections of different moulding profiles and
the appropriate nail placement for each.*

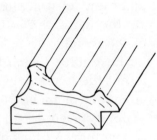
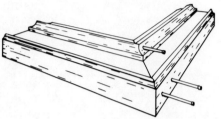

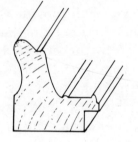
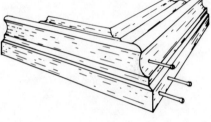

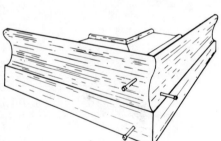

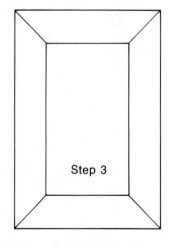

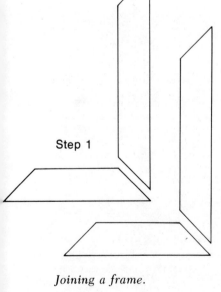

Step 1

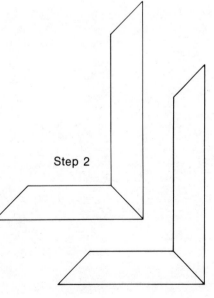

Step 2

Step 3

Joining a frame.

stick back in the vise in the same position and secure it again. Since you lined it up perfectly, it will go right back in place and fit this time.

Next, nail the pieces together. If you aren't experienced with a hammer, drill holes in the wood first. This is especially helpful if the wood is hard, such as walnut, oak, or maple. Choose a drill bit that is slightly thinner than the nail you are using. This will allow for a nice tight fit. It is not necessary to drill the hole as far as the nail will penetrate the wood; just a hole to get the nail started will be fine. About ½'' into the wood should be sufficient.

Now hammer the nail into the wood. The design of some mouldings does not permit you to hammer the nail or brad close to the wood. In this case use a nail set to tap the nail into the wood and then set it about $^1/_{16}$'' into the wood. This will let you putty the nail later with a substance close in color to the finish of the wood.

After you have joined each long stick to a short stick, you are ready to put the two halves together. Since the vise holds the frame a couple of inches off the table, you will need to support the opposite corner of the frame while you join the whole frame together. A block of wood or something similar in height to the vise will provide adequate support for the frame while the other side is being joined.

Finally, fill in the cracks and nailholes. Take a child's crayon in the appropriate color and scrape some off around the nailhole with a utility knife or single-edge razor blade and rub it in the nailholes with a putty stick. Wipe off any excess with a cloth. For the four corner cracks, scrape off some crayon with a utility knife over the crack and push in the crayon with a putty stick.

mounting a picture

TOOLS AND MATERIALS:
  spray glue (3M Sprament)
  soft cloth
  pencil
  brayer

OPTIONAL:
  iron
  clean rag
  distilled water

Definition: To mount a picture is to glue it down to a piece of compressed cardboard or a stiff, flat, smooth surface (usually a paper product) so that the print or photo will lay flat in the frame.

A print of normal thickness can usually be flattened out and fitted in the frame without having to go to the trouble of mounting it. More importantly, you destroy the value of the picture when you mount. If at all possible, it is best not to mount. We never know how valuable something might be in the future.

There are certain items you *never* mount. Documents such as diplomas, certificates, important business transactions, and famous signatures should never be mounted. You should also never mount fine, expensive art prints. Use the flattening method described here and then follow the procedure described in the section on conservation mounting.

Preparation: You can keep your print between two pieces of cardboard rather than rolled in a tube. If it has been rolled, it will take about a week for the cellular structure to reshape itself to a flattened shape. After you have reshaped the structure you may still have some wrinkles you need to work out. The following method *cannot* be used on photos, and we never recommend it on valuable artwork or a signed lithograph. Posters that will be hung without glass, and pictures and prints that have gotten very wrinkled are good candidates for mounting.

Working from the back of the print, rub and dab a little distilled water on the wrinkle. Use a clean washrag. Now you are ready to apply low heat.

Lay the print face down on an ironing board, lay a paper towel (or a thin, clean cloth) across the wrinkle, and lightly place the iron on top of the paper. This will evaporate the moisture that is in the print and flatten out the wrinkle. Be sure you are working from the back of the print. Now you are ready to mount.

As always when spraying, you should do it in a room other than where you are working. Lay out newspaper so you will not spray the floor or table.

When you mount anything smaller than 12″×16″ you have to spray only the back of your photo or print. In mounting anything larger than that you will need to spray both surfaces— that is, the back of the print or photo, and the front of the mounting board. If the picture is to have a mat, be sure to leave enough mounting board around the picture so it will go all the way to the edge of the mat when you place the mat on top of the picture. If there is excess mounting board after laying the mat on top of it you can trim the excess off.

For a 12″×16″ or smaller print: Lay the picture face down on paper (in a separate room if possible), and spray the back evenly. Allow the glue to get very gummy and sticky. Take the picture into the workroom and lay it (glue side down) on the mounting board. Take a clean, soft cloth and dab the picture down on the mounting board. With your brayer, roll the pic-

Spray-gluing the back of an inexpensive print or poster

ture. Always roll from the center out and be sure to use a cover sheet.

On sizes larger than 12″×16″: Lay the picture on the board and mark off the dimensions so you will know exactly where to spray. You have allowed extra mounting board on the picture if it will have a mat. Now you are ready to spray in a room with good ventilation other than your workroom.

Lay the mounting board (with marked side up) and the picture (face down) on newspapers and begin to spray. We cover the surfaces completely, first horizontally and then vertically. When both surfaces are very tacky and gummy, take your pieces back to the workroom and place the two sprayed sides together, taking care to lay the picture within the marked dimensions. Dab the picture with a soft cloth, then roll down the picture with a brayer.

DRY MOUNTING

You can also mount with dry-mount tissue, which is available at photo stores. Cut a long, narrow strip of it for each side of the top edge of the picture. Position the tissue on top of your mounting board, then place your picture over that. Now put a clean piece of paper over the print as a cover sheet, be sure that the picture is centered on the mounting board, and place a weight on it so it doesn't move. Now heat up an iron on low heat (about 200°) and when it is hot enough to melt the dry-mount tissue (test on a scrap) run the tip of the iron over the cover sheet where the tissue is located. For photographs, you'll need to use a pressure-sensitive dry-mount tissue.

picture
dry-mount tissue
mounting board

stretching a canvas

If you paint, you'll not only want to know how to make your own frame, but also how to stretch your own canvas. There are a lot of advantages to doing this yourself.* It is less expensive, and for the artist this is a definite advantage. Once you have learned how to stretch your own, the quality will be better than you find in a prestretched canvas. You can also use money you save to buy a higher-quality canvas. If you need to ship or transport a used canvas, it can be taken off the strips and shipped that way. It is then less susceptible to puncture. After it reaches its destination, it can be restretched. (This may be difficult to do if the canvas is very old or heavily textured.)

You can pick linen canvas or cotton canvas. Linen is a high-quality canvas and should be used with high-quality artists' paints. Cotton is more popular because it is more economical. Linen materials do not stretch as much as cotton, so you will find it more difficult to stretch linen canvas.

It is far easier to purchase precut strips in the approximate length you need than even to consider cutting them yourself. They come in different lengths, graduating by 2'', and are easy to assemble: The slotted ends simply fit together. You would save only a small amount of money doing it yourself, and it is not worth the time and trouble. In addition, you would not have the little wedges or keys you receive when you buy precut strips. These wedges are hammered into the slots on all four corners when the canvas has reacted to time and the environment and has started to sag. (When you insert the wedges, lay a small piece of cardboard on the canvas so that you don't dent it.)

TOOLS AND MATERIALS:
  stretcher pliers
  staple gun or tacks
  carpenter's square
  canvas (cotton or linen)
  stretcher strips

*If you do purchase prestretched canvas never consider anything larger than 24''×30''. Anything larger will warp and you will not be happy with it. (If you *must* purchase a larger one, be sure it has heavy duty strips.) Once you get the knack of stretching, you will want to stretch all of your own canvas regardless of size.

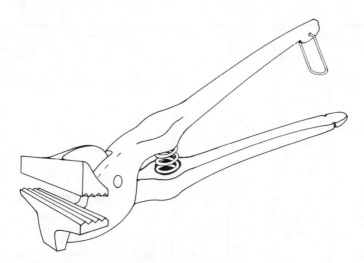

Stretcher pliers used in stretching canvas.

Assemble your stretcher strips so that the corners are snug. Now you must be sure that the stretcher frame is in square — that is, that each corner is at a 90° angle. There are two ways to do this: (1) Check the outside dimensions of the strips with a carpenter square, or (2) measure the diagonals of the stretcher frame. They must be of equal length for the stretcher frame to be in square. If it is still out of square, then the strips are not together right and must be adjusted. Move them around until the frame is in square.

If the new frame is larger than 30″×40″, you'll need to brace it. Be sure to do this before you put on the canvas. If one brace is needed, cut 1″×2″ for the smallest inside dimension. Cut the length as close as possible for a perfect fit. When you install it, be sure it fits as far to the back as possible so there is no chance of the brace touching the canvas. If the frame is larger than 36″×48″ it will need cross bracing. Cut a brace to fit across the width of the canvas and then a piece to fit on either side of the brace. Put glue on either end of the brace. Use 16-gauge nails and angle them through the strip and into the brace. Two nails per side will work. For added strength use one nail from the brace into the strip.

Measure the strips after you have added these braces, to be sure you have not knocked the stretcher strips out of square.

Now you are ready to stretch. Leave at least 1½″–2½″ of excess canvas around the strips to grasp. For example, for a 30″×40″ canvas the perimeter of the canvas must be at least 33″×43″. You can staple it either on the side or on the back of the strips. If the side of the canvas is to be painted, you will need to staple on the back. If it doesn't matter, you can try both ways to see which is easier for you. It may depend on the size canvas you are stretching.

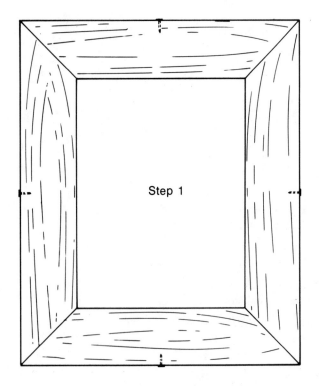

Step 1

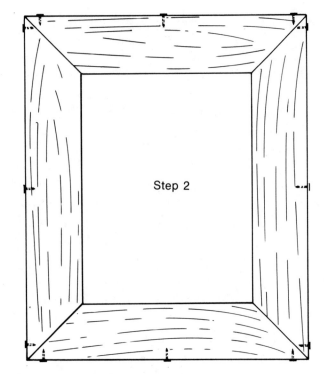

Step 2

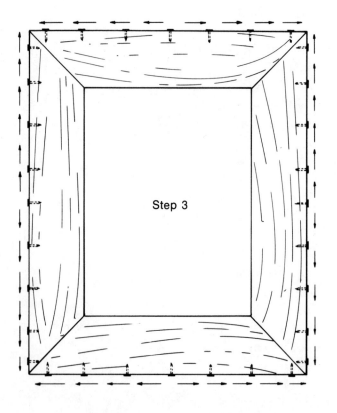

Step 3

Note gradual brad or staple placement in Steps 1, 2, and 3.

Lay the canvas on a clean, flat surface. If the canvas is primed, be sure that the primed side is face down. Lay the joined stretcher strips on top of the canvas. Fold one edge of the canvas around a strip (on the shorter side, if there is one) and place two tacks or staples close together in the middle of the strip. Using stretcher pliers, grip the canvas on the opposite side and tug until a visible crease appears. Place two more tacks or staples close together in the middle of this strip. Now, moving to the long stretcher strip, grasp the canvas with the pliers and tug until you have a pryamid-shaped crease in the canvas. Again place two tacks or staples in the middle of the strip. Now move to the fourth side and tug until you have a diamond-shaped crease in the canvas. Again place two staples in the middle of the strip.

Place two tacks or staples at each corner of the canvas while pulling the canvas taut. This will anchor it and hold excess canvas taut. Working out from the center, and proceeding gradually to the corners, put in a few tacks or staples at a time on each strip. Do not try to tack or staple all of one side at a time. When you get 2½" from the corner, remove the anchoring tacks or staples. Examine the canvas to be sure there are not any unwanted creases. Finish off the corners using a hospital-bed fold. Do not trim off excess canvas. At some point in the future it may need to be restretched and you will need the excess canvas.

putting it
all together

The frame is joined, the mat and glass are cut, and you are now entering the final stage of picture framing, called fitting. Following are the basic instructions for fitting an unmounted print with a mat under glass. These are followed by special instructions for variations you might have: mounted prints under glass, prints with mats on top of the glass, etc.

BASIC FITTING

TOOLS AND MATERIALS:
  high-quality gummed brown paper tape
  eraser
  hair dryer
  clean paintbrush or whisk broom
  backing board
  white glue
  glass cleaner and paper towels
  brown wrapping paper
  brads
  crayon
  nails
  hammer
  wire cutters
  putty stick
  utility knife or single-edge razor
  corrugated cardboard
  two-faced tape

First, clean your glass. If you don't have access to a glass cleaner, you can make one that will work very well. Mix 5% rubbing alcohol (isopropyl), 5% ammonia, and 90% water. Clean both sides of the glass using this and paper towels or clean rags. We always keep an extra spray bottle of water to give the glass a final water rinse to make sure all the glass cleaner is removed.

68

If you are cleaning acrylic instead of glass, purchase an acrylic cleaner at a plastics supply house. Use a soft cotton rag and wash the surface of the acrylic thoroughly on both surfaces (front and back). In addition to cleaning the acrylic it will also eliminate static from the surface so it will not attract dust. Any other type of cleaner can scratch acrylic. Also, the rinsing action is not necessary when the acrylic cleaner has been used.

Then sweep out the lip of the frame with a whisk broom to remove any residue or dust that might have gathered.

You will need a backing board directly behind the picture. Cut one to the same outside dimension as the mat. Many different kinds of boards can be used as the backing board. They are listed here in the order of highest quality on down.

Rag board: Produced from pure cotton fibers. Mainly used in conservation mounting. The most expensive backing board available.

Illustration board: This is a fine sheet of rag board paper sized to the top of a lower-quality and less-refined wood pulp board. The rag-covered side will be touching the back of the picture.

Foam core: A very rigid, inert board having a plastic foam center and a wood pulp white surface on the front and back. It reacts like a sponge if squeezed tightly and will be permanently damaged if this is done, so examine the board closely before fitting.

Wood pulp board: This is usually used in manufacturing mat boards and will have a color on one side. If it has a bright color on one side use the opposite side, as the bright colors tend to fade faster into the print. Buy white board. You may have an extra piece of mat board left over from the one you cut for the print; this is suitable for a regular picture-framing technique.

Newsboard: This is made of reprocessed newspaper, and is gray.

Poster board: Purchase the thick type (at least $1/16''$).

Chipboard and Upsom board: Of lower quality than the others but still much better than corrugated cardboard.

Set the print on the backing board and place the mat over the picture. Center your picture under the mat. Remove the mat and with the brown gummed tape, tape the top of the print to the backing board. Do not tape the sides or bottom of the print, because this will not allow movement in the picture. Different temperatures and humidities will cause movement in the picture. (Only fine museums have a completely controlled environment.)

Once the print is attached to the backing board, attach the mat to the backing board. If the outside dimension of the print is smaller than the outside dimension of the mat, you can use two-faced tape on the backing board. Place the tape around the perimeter of the board, keeping as far from the print as possible. Place the mat on top of the tape and secure the mat by hammering the top of the mat with your clean fist. Quite a few prints are designed with a border that will be very similar to the borders you want, and you should make them the same size if possible. For example, if your print is surrounded by a 3″ white border and you want to have a 3″ mat, the print will fit nicely in the frame; you don't have to tape it to the backing board. Avoid trimming the print, because this will ruin its market value. You never know what will be considered valuable in the future (if it isn't already valuable).

Place your clean glass in the frame, then add the matted picture face down. Next add cardboard cut the same outside dimension as the mat to buffer the picture from the climate. It will keep the picture from buckling. With the frame firmly braced against a piece of wood clamped or nailed to the table, place a couple of brads flush against the board. Hammer the brads into the inside of the frame perpendicular to the moulding. Nail them in deep enough to have the brads in firmly where they cannot be pulled out with your fingers. Turn the frame over to see if any dust or specks of dirt are caught between the glass and the picture. If there is dust, remove the nails and blow it out with a hair dryer, or brush it out with a clean, dry paintbrush. With everything back in the frame, nail brads every 2″–3″ around the back of the frame (perpendicular to the inside of the frame) to hold the cardboard in snugly. When all the brads are in, depress them somewhat with a hammer or wire cutters.

Seal the cardboard to the frame with gummed brown paper tape to keep dust and bugs out. You can add a final dust cover or backing cover. Squeeze out a thin line of white glue around the outside perimeter of the back of the frame. Smooth out the glue with a clean brush or your finger. Lay out the paper and smooth it over the glue. (Almost any kind of paper can be used except newspaper. It is too thin and will age rapidly. Brown wrapping paper is best.) A single-edge razor blade can be used to trim off any excess paper so it won't show over the edge of the frame.

VARIATIONS IN FITTING

MOUNTED PICTURES WITH MATS UNDER GLASS

If the mounted picture is not already attached to the mat, you must do it. Apply two-faced tape on the mounting board around the picture, being careful to keep it away from the picture. Now lay the back of the mat on the picture, and the two-faced tape will hold them sufficiently. If there is any mounting board sticking out from the mat, trim it off, utilizing the spring clamp, metal ruler, and utility knife.

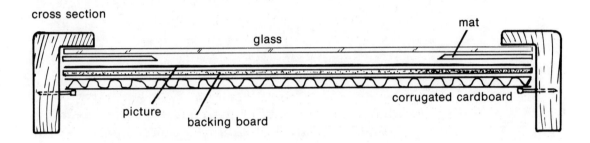

cross section
glass
mat
picture
backing board
corrugated cardboard

MOUNTED OR UNMOUNTED PRINTS WITHOUT MATS

Proceed as in the basic instructions, minus the mat. If the frame is deep, you can use corrugated cardboard as a filler.

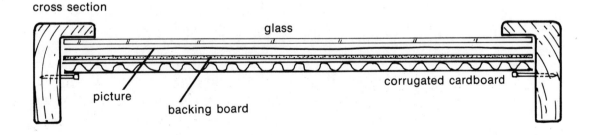

cross section
glass
picture
backing board
corrugated cardboard

MOUNTED OR UNMOUNTED PRINTS WITH
MAT ON TOP OF GLASS

When you have a fabric mat, you usually want to put it on top of the glass. The mat is more attractive and much richer-looking that way than pressed under the glass. But there are exceptions to every rule, and when using a very pale or white fabric we recommend putting it under the glass to prevent the fabric from getting dirty. Also consider the intended location of the picture. A picture will get more abuse in a kitchen, breakfast room, or bathroom than in a bedroom or a living room. Smoke will affect unprotected mats adversely. Sometimes you can place a paper mat on the outside of the glass. We have a watercolor that has two mats on the outside. One is paper and the other is fabric. After 3½ years there has been no noticeable wear and tear on the paper mat.

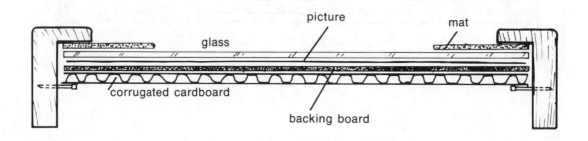

First, attach the mat to the glass. Cut the glass ⅛" smaller all the way around. This will help to prevent breakage when the mat, glass, and print are being nailed into the frame. Usually you have the mat buffering the glass, but in this case it is right against the frame, so you must take greater care.

Lay the mat down on a flat, clean location. If the mat is wide, apply white glue in a thin line about ¾" away from the inner opening, and in a second line about ¾" away from the outside perimeter of the mat. Place a few dabs of glue between the two borders of glue so that when flattened they will be about the size of a nickel. Smooth out the glue with a paintbrush or your finger. Be sure there are no globs of glue on the inner border of the mat that could squeeze out when the glass is laid on top. If your mat is too narrow to allow two lines of glue, you can use one line in the middle of the mat. Follow the same procedure for smoothing out the glue. Now you are ready to lay your clean glass on the back of the mat. Wait at least an hour—overnight, if possible—and the mat and glass will be ready to fit into the frame.

If the print is unmounted you need to attach it to a backing board. Attach your print to the board with brown gummed tape. Two pieces at the top of the print border will suffice. Place the mat and glass on top of the picture, centering as necessary.

Place the frame face down on the table. Lay in the mat with glass attached, the picture, and the backing board. The frame needs to be snugly supported against a piece of wood with a C clamp or a spring clamp, or it should be nailed to the table. This will keep the side of the frame you are working on from breaking apart when you are hammering. Nail small brads 2″–3″ apart all the way around the frame. These brads should be flush against the backing board, holding it tightly into the frame. If the frame is deep you can add a couple of pieces of cardboard of the same outside dimensions as the mat. Only two or three brads per side are needed for this layer.

Nailing brads into the back of the frame to hold the picture in place. Note temporary bar held by C clamps.

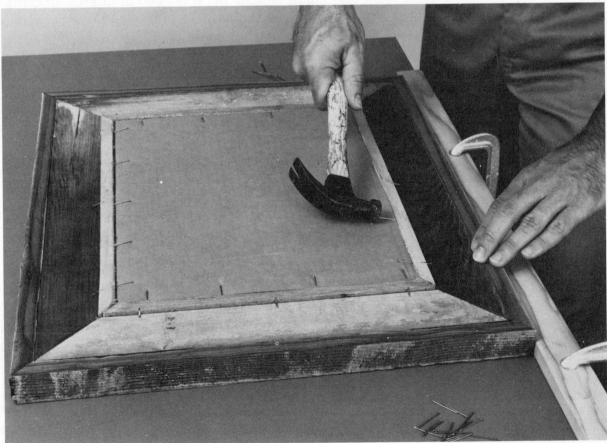

Seal the frame, cover the back with brown wrapping paper, and fill in the nailholes and cracks (see page 60).

FITTING A CANVAS

In our opinion a stretched canvas is the most proven medium for art and one of the most expensive. The correct process of fitting it in the frame can prevent warping and wrinkles in the canvas.

Place the canvas in the frame and nail thin brads 4″–5″ apart around the back of the frame. Bend them over so they are just touching the back of the stretcher strips. This will allow the canvas to move with the changing environment. *Do not nail into the stretcher strips.*

Once in a while you will want to use glass over a canvas. If a valuable and/or old work of art is going to be displayed in a public place such as a library or a restaurant, we advise using glass as a protection. This could even be necessary in your home if you hang a valuable piece in a precarious spot.

Acrylic is best and is the least distracting. It is also less apt to break and injure the art. You will need to insert some strips of balsa wood between the canvas and the acrylic so the acrylic does not touch the art.

A piece of cardboard can be placed in the back of the frame to protect the canvas from dust and bugs and from being torn or pierced. A few brads on each side will hold this cardboard in place. Be sure to nail the brads into the frame. Finally for your best protection and a finished look, apply the paper dust cover, as described in the basic instructions.

Once in a while you will have a canvas that protrudes from back of the frame because the canvas is deeper than the frame. Cut a piece of cardboard about 1″–1¼″ larger than the canvas;

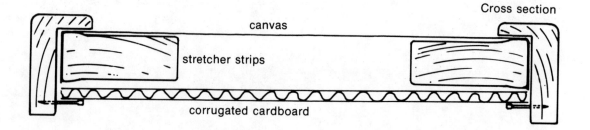

Cross section

canvas

stretcher strips

corrugated cardboard

nail or staple the cardboard to the edge of the frame. The cardboard will then angle down over the edge of the canvas to the frame. Before nailing the cardboard, cut out the corners where they would double up.

There is one other alternative. If the cardboard does not coordinate with the design and construction of your frame, you can use a piece of fabric, perhaps one that coordinates with the picture or your furniture. The main idea is to protect the picture, so even a heavy or a doubled piece of paper will do.

Check the next section on picture hanging for the specific method of hanging your picture; be sure to put your hardware into the frame and not the stretcher strips.

picture hanging

The proper combination of hangers on the wall and on the back of the frame are of utmost importance to ensure safe hanging of your picture. Everyday wear and tear, door shutting, walking across the room, or even brushing up against a picture will take their toll on improper hanging implements and could result in a picture falling off the wall. In addition, you want to ensure that the picture will be level.

Descriptions of various types of hangers you can use follow. Letters A through E designate the kinds of hangers that attach to the wall: Nos. 1 through 4 indicate hangers that attach to the frame. The following chart will make it easy for you to know what combinations of hangers to use in particular situations.

HANGERS FOR THE WALL

A. This is a small hanger that can support up to 10 lbs. However, using two will keep the picture from swaying. Hanger A can be used with frame hangers 1, 2, 3, and 4. Screw eyes and wire are used for most pictures in professional frame shops. If you decide to use two A hangers, place them a quar-

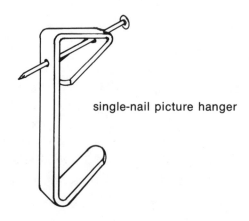

single-nail picture hanger

PICTURE HANGING CHART

WEIGHT OF PICTURE	TYPE OF WALL			
	SHEETROCK	WOOD PANELING	BRICK	PLASTER
up to 10 lbs.	A-1* A-2* A-3	A-1* A-2† A-3	E-1*; nailed in brick	A-1*; drill tiny hole
11–25 lbs.	A-2† B-1*	A-2† B-1*	E-1* D-1* E-1*; in brick	D-1* D-4† over 20 lbs.; use D-4
26–54 lbs.	A-4† B-1*	A-4† B-1*	D-1* D-4† over 40 lbs., use D-4	D-1* D-4† over 40 lbs., use D-4
55–74 lbs.	B-1† C-4†	B-1†	D-4†	D-4†
75 lbs. or over	C-4†	B-4†	D-4†	D-4†

*Two hangers on the wall are preferable to keep the picture from swaying.
†Two hangers on the wall are mandatory to keep the picture from swaying and for strength. This applies to more permanent hanging, since the two holes in the wall will have to be repaired if the picture is moved.

ter of the way in from where the outer edge of the frame will be. Of course, you will nail this hanger into the wall, so you must mark the outside measurement of the frame on the wall. You can mark it with masking tape, which won't mar the wall.

If you use frame hanger 2, you must use two A hangers, as there is no wire. Turn the screw eyes horizontally. This is also ideal when you use glass mats, as there is no wire to show through. You will also use two A hangers with frame hanger 4.

B. This hanger can be used with frame hangers 1 or 4. If you need more permanent hanging, use two B's. Place one halfway between the center of the picture and the outside of the frame on either side. For example, on a 20″-wide frame the hangers would be 5″ from either edge. This will keep the picture from swaying and give it more stable and permanent hanging.

If you happen to get the hook a little high, you can eliminate the problem by doing one of two things: (1) If the height is just a bit off, merely roll a piece of tape around the hanger on the back of the frame, or (2) unscrew the hanger and either raise or lower.

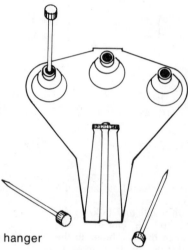

triple-nail picture hanger

C. A molly-bolt is used with frame hanger 4 and on sheetrock with heavy pictures and framed mirrors. When buying a molly-bolt be sure to get the type with the flat end. (There is one with a pointed end that can cause problems—sometimes the mechanism breaks and is stuck in the wall.) Drill a hole the same diameter as the molly-bolt shaft and push the molly-bolt into that hole. Turn the screw clockwise until the tension ceases. Do not force the screw. Now the screw can be turned counterclockwise until the screwhead sticks away from the wall from ¼″ to ³⁄₈″, and you are ready to hang the picture on it. It is easier if you have two people to hang the picture on molly-bolts. Let one person get one hanger on; then the other person can get the other on.

molly-bolt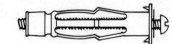

D. This lead sinker is also available in plastic, but the lead is more durable. This is used with hangers 1 and 4 in brick or plaster walls. Before you can install the sinker you must drill a hole. For brick, use a carbide steel masonry bit—you should be able to drill into either the brick or the mortar (that stuff found between the bricks). Use a drill bit that is about $\frac{1}{16}''$ smaller than the lead sinker, and drill at the desired position. Be sure you drill the hole deep enough to swallow the whole sinker. Now insert the sinker into this hole until the front of the sinker is flush with the front of the brick. When the screws are into the sinker, the walls of the lead will expand and will be snugly wedged in the brick or plaster.

lead sinker
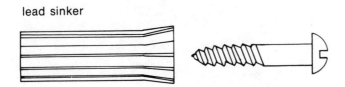

E. This is a special hanger made for brick and used with hanger 1. Find the right spot, place the hanger on it, and hammer four carbide nails (already attached to the hanger) into the brick. Again, two can be used for a more permanent hanging.

brick-wall hanger

HANGERS FOR THE BACK OF THE FRAME

1. Screw eyes and wire, used with wall hangers A, B, C, D, and E. Take an ice pick or an awl and start a hole about a third of the way down the back of the frame (for instance, if the frame is 18'' high, place the screw eye 6'' from the top). For leverage you can use the ice pick or a long nail through the center of the screw eye and tighten it until the base of the screw eye is embedded in the wood.

When you wrap the wire around the screw eye, be sure to

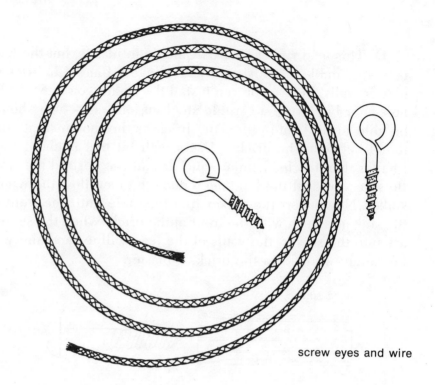

screw eyes and wire

make a no-slip knot. Take one end of the wire and place it from the inside of the screw eye to the outside, then back under the lead-in wire, back around the outside, and through the screw eye. Now twist the wire tightly and snugly around the main wire. Do the same to the other side.

2. If you have a frame with screw eyes already attached to the frame and wire running across the back, simply clip the wire off with wire cutters and turn the screw eyes horizontally. Put the picture in the desired position and press the frame (where the screw eyes are located) into the sheetrock or paneling. Pull the frame away and you will see you have made two depressions. Put a level on top of the frame to be absolutely certain it is level. Take the A hangers and line up the bottom of the hanger with the depression in the wall and hammer in. Now hang the picture on the hanger and the job is done. You must use two A's. You will never have to adjust the picture.

3. Sawtooth hanger. This hanger is basically used for small pictures. It should not be seen from the top of the picture. If the frame is too thin or weighs 5 lbs. or less, you could use nails instead of A's. Two sawtooth hangers are good when you have a glass mat.

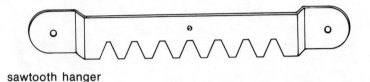

sawtooth hanger

4. This is a mirror hanger and is basically used on pictures weighing 20 lbs. or more. You must use two wall hangers with this. Do not use wire across the back, as it will cause the hangers to twist inward and split the wood; many pictures have been ruined this way. It can be used with hangers B, C, and D. If it is used with B, you must be sure it does not show from the front. When you use it with C or D, make sure all the measurements are accurate before installation in the wall. If the picture doesn't hang perfectly you can either roll a little tape around the mirror hanger to raise one side, or adjust the hanger itself.

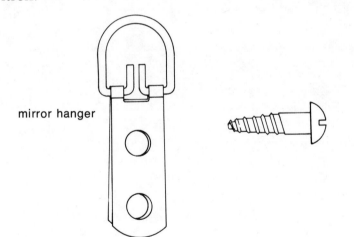

mirror hanger

III
WHEN YOU'RE HAVING IT FRAMED: A GUIDE TO DESIGN

WHILE IT IS NOT really as simple as A-B-C, we hope that this will serve as a basic guide to help you in choosing a frame, mat, glass, and the proper mounting for your artwork.

canvas or
canvas board

White stretched canvas is the highest quality of art media, while canvas board is of very low quality and tends to buckle easily.

Glass: This is usually not used on a canvas, except when the canvas is exposed in a public place. A library, restaurant, or such may warrant glass. If it is a very valuable piece, read the section on conservation framing for canvas. (See page 179.)

Liner: For a canvas, mats are not desirable, as they are made of paper and/or fabric and are too flimsy to hold the weight of the canvas, unless it is heavily braced (even then we've seen them in need of repair after a couple of years). Therefore we always advise use of a liner. A liner is a wooden moulding used inside the outer frame. The usual liner sizes are 1/2″–4″. The liner can be covered with fabric, stained, or painted to a desired effect. An inner 1/2″ liner can be used on the inside of a larger liner—say 2½″–3″.

Mounting: Your canvas will need to be stretched if it isn't stretched already. If you can't get the frame you want at this time, the canvas can be wrapped around the back of the stretcher strips so that the staples do not show. Attach screw eyes and wire to the back of the frame and you can hang the picture up until you are able to get the frame you want. Art done on canvas board needs no mounting as it is already on a stiff board that is suitable for framing.

Frame: There are several combinations available for the stretched canvas:

A narrow outside frame with a 3″ liner and another ½″ liner on the inside. Be sure the outside frame is deep enough for the thickness of the canvas.

A 3″-wide frame with a ½″–1″ liner on the inside.

A plain wood stripping to be tacked to the side of the stretcher strips. The stripping can be of natural wood or wood side with a gold or silver top. We do not recommend this on fine artwork.

A simple cap frame (one with a narrow top and deep sides) is also suitable.

On canvas board, a simple cap frame is most suitable.

documents

A document is a very personal possession and should be framed with conservation mounting and framing.

Acrylic: It can be an ultraviolet-filtered acrylic, as the inks on a document tend to fade easily, and this type of acrylic will filter out that damaging ray. Remember, all light fades pieces. This type of acrylic should be used for more important documents such as college degrees or old family heirlooms that have never been properly framed.

Mat: Acrylic should not touch the document so be sure to use a mat. We prefer a straight-cut mat here, as the dark inner core of a bevel-cut mat does not always coordinate with the white or off-white in the document (the exception to this would be an all-rag board mat that is the same color all the way through the inner core of the mat). A fabric mat is especially nice for a top mat with a ⅛″ contrasting color on the inside. We prefer to use natural colors such as grays, browns, gold, or even black on documents. If the document is a college degree and the school colors would work, you can use them on the inner mat. The size of the document will determine the size of the mat. The border of the mat can be 1½″–3″. If there is a color in the document, you can pick it up in the ⅛″ mat.

Mounting: Do not permanently mount a certificate or document. Use the hinging process described in conservation framing. If you don't conservation frame the document, still do not mount it permanently. Instead, use brown gummed tape (as opposed to a pressure-sensitive tape like masking tape).

Frame: The importance of the document should be reflected by the frame design. If you want an ornate frame, choose a sculptured antique gold or silver one, possibly with a black band, with the moulding not over 1½″ in width. A simple frame is very much in order with a document. A walnut or a black frame can be very tastefully done. If you've just graduated and you want your diploma inexpensively framed, choose a ½″ or ¾″ black or brown moulding, but don't have the document mounted and be sure that no corrugated cardboard is put directly behind the document. If you want something extra special, see the glass mat project, page 129.

art on masonite

Glass: none

Mat: none

Liner: You can use a liner; for example, 1″ frame with a 3″ liner and a ½″ liner on the inside of that. Or you can use a simple cap frame. You can also choose a 3″ frame with a ¼″–1″ liner.

mirrors

Glass: Mirrors need no glass over them.

Mat: A mat is not strong enough to support the weight of a mirror.

Mounting: Be sure to place a piece of cardboard behind the mirror before nailing it into the frame.

Frame and liner: You can use a frame and liner with a mirror. Usually a wide, ornate frame with a ³⁄₄″ or 1″ fabric-covered liner is appropriate and structurally sound. A liner is not necessary but can add to the beauty of the framed mirror. You can use practically any coordinating liner-frame combination on a mirror, since you are not working to coordinate with the mirror but rather with your decor. A wide wooden frame or a wide contemporary metal frame can be used. Be sure to use a wood-covered metal frame, since a plain metal frame could chip the mirror.

Fitting: Be sure to blacken the inside lip of the frame; otherwise the inside lip will be reflected in the mirror, and the rawness of the inside of the frame will show.

needlepoint
and crewel

Glass: Glass can be placed over needlepoint and crewel for protection; however, these types really look better without glass. Here we have the problem of deciding between looks and the longevity of the artwork. In ten years the piece with glass will look better than the piece without glass. Acrylic will pick up lint from the yarn and will tend to look dirty. Nonglare

This wedding needlepoint by Patricia Pike features the bride and groom's initials and the wedding date. A small gold inside liner, a green linen-covered mat and a gold leaf frame make it a gift you would be proud to give or receive.

glass can be used only if the glass is no more than $1/16''$ from the needlework.

Liner: A liner looks better than a mat with needlework. A liner is not necessary, but it keeps the glass off the textured stitches and avoids a squashed look. Use a $1/2''$–$3''$ liner. If the liner is $3/4''$ or smaller, use a frame at least twice as wide as the liner. If the liner is wider than $1''$, a simple cap moulding about $1/2''$ wide and $1\frac{3}{8}''$ deep works well. Again, the fine-weaved linens and cottons, as well as velvet, do best on this liner.

Mounting: A needlework will always be stretched over a $3/16''$ Upsom board or stretcher strips. We prefer the Upsom board. Spray glue a piece of four-ply rag board to the surface of the Upsom board and you have a conservation effect, in that the acid from the Upsom board will not touch the needlework. White felt can also be spray glued to the top of the Upsom board to absorb any knubby fabric or knots on the back of some needlework. This white felt is of good quality and has a conservation mounting effect as well.

Frame: Use a frame at least twice as wide as the liner if the liner is $3/4''$ or less wide, otherwise a cap moulding can be used. If a liner is not used, be sure to use a spacer between the glass and the needlework. These are narrow strips of mat board cut to about $1/8''$–$1/16''$ that will be glued to the back of the glass along the edge where it will be hidden by the frame.

pastels and charcoal drawings

Glass: Even though acrylic will give you the best clarity and is less likely to break, you cannot use it on pastels and charcoals because its static nature will actually lift the pastel or charcoal off the paper. You can use regular glass on a single or double mat. You can use nonglare glass on a single mat or if the fabric mat is placed on top of the glass, with the rag board mat (which will not show) placed between the drawing and the glass. *The glass must never touch a pastel or charcoal drawing.*

Mat: You can place a fabric mat on top of the glass. Fine-weaved fabrics, linens, cotton combinations, and silks all look fine here. You can also use a 1/8″ inside mat. Be sure to put a rag mat under the glass to keep the drawing from touching the glass.

Liner: A fabric-covered liner with the same fabric as the mat and used on the inside of the frame can be very nice and accentuate the importance of your drawing.

Mounting: The drawing should be hinged at the top using a rag board as a backing board. (The drawing will be hinged to the rag board.)

Frame: A moulding of about 3/4″–1¼″ is usually used in combination with a mat and/or mat-liner combination.

photographs

Glass: If the photograph is single-matted you may use nonglare glass or acrylic. If it is double-matted under the glass, use regular glass or acrylic. If double-matted on the top of the glass with a rag board mat between the photo and the glass, you can also use any of the three. You should use a mat on the photo to separate the glass and the photo, or the photo will eventually stick to the glass. Glossy photos will stick to glass very easily, but matte-finished photos seem to avoid the sticking. If you have an expensive portrait-type photo done by a top photographer, you should definitely consider an ultraviolet-filter acrylic. All light fades pictures; color photos seem to be especially susceptible to sunlight and fluorescent lighting. Avoid hanging near sunlight and use the ultraviolet-filter acrylic.

Mat: Use either a single or a double mat on photos. Fabric mats are also very suitable. Imitation suede, fine-weaved linens, silks, velvet, and cotton combinations all work well. Avoid knubby materials and heavy-weave fabrics such as burlap, for they detract from the photo.

Liner: A liner is very suitable for a photo-portrait. Again, use a fine-weaved material and stay away from the heavy ones. A liner will help to keep the glass away from the photo. If you use the liner or the mat on top, you will need to use spacers to keep the glass off the picture. (See the section on framing needlework, page 136.)

Mounting: In mounting a photo always use the dry mount technique. Recently the 3M Company has come out with a dry mounting tissue that is pressure-sensitive rather than heat-sensitive. This allows you to dry mount at home rather than depending on an expensive heat press. It is most effective on photos 14"×18" or smaller. Most quality photo portraits are dry mounted by the photo company.

Frame: Choose a frame that will complement the picture and reflect the general mood of the picture. For a rustic photo choose a wooden frame—possibly a barnwood frame. For a traditional photo choose a narrow moulding with a wide mat—for example, a 3" mat and a 3/4" moulding on an 11"×14" photo. All the metal mouldings available in a variety of colors are appropriate here. On a portrait photo a small liner 3/4" with a wide frame (2"–3") is appropriate, especially for a 14"×18" or a 16"×20" photo.

posters

If you have a poster you want to keep for a long time, frame it as a regular print. If you have a poster that will be used for just a short period in a child's life, only the simplest framing is in order—no glass, no mat, no liner.

Mounting: Preferably a foam core board. If you can't get this, check the chart on mounting board (see page 69) and find a suitable backing board. Since there is no glass or mat, you can use a simple frame. If it is larger than 24″×36″, at least a ³/₄″ moulding should be used. The metal mouldings available in a variety of colors work well with posters.

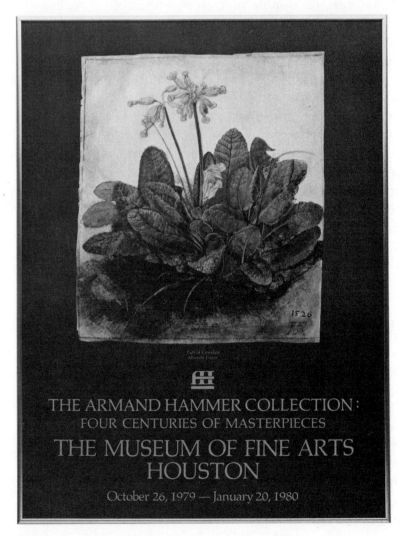

This poster meant a lot to us so we used a metal frame with glass to preserve it.

prints

SIGNED AND NUMBERED

A signed and numbered print, a seriograph, lithograph, etching, or any print that is valuable to you should have a conservation frame (see page 171).

Glass: The glass can be ultraviolet acrylic if it will be hung in ultraviolet light (fluorescent or sunlight through a window). If not, you can use regular glass; nonglare glass if a double mat is not being used. The farther the print is from nonglare glass the fuzzier the print will appear.

Mat: You can use double mats here with contrasting colors. In most instances a bevel would be nice. For a high-quality print use only four-ply rag (which is not colorful, but it protects the print very well). If color and conservation are important, use the four-ply rag under the glass next to the print, a fabric mat on top of the glass with a $1/8''-1/4''$-size inner mat, and the fabric mat any size you choose. The four-ply mat will not show, and the double mat will be on the outside of the glass. This also lets you use nonglare glass, because the glass will only be one mat away from the print.

Mounting: A valuable print should be conservation mounted—that is, hinged (see page 172)—on the back of 100% rag board.

Frame: Choose the frame that fits the feeling of the picture best.

REGULAR PRINTS

If you have purchased a decorative print and paid only $1.50 to $15 for it, you may want to use a decorative mat not of conservation quality. In these types of prints, lower-quality paper and lower-quality printing were employed; therefore the print won't last as long as an expensive print. We own many of these types of prints and dearly love them. We recently paid $3.00 for a $22'' \times 28''$ Mark Rothko print at the Museum of Fine Arts in Houston. The print is framed in an off-white mat and acrylic frame. We are careful not to expose it to the sunlight.

Glass: Regular or nonglare (as long as you don't have a double mat).

Mat: With a regular print it is kind of fun to choose a mat because you do not have to worry about acidity of the mat and you can be as decorative as you want. (See "Variations on a Mat," page 35.)

Mounting: A print should never have to be mounted. As long as it has been stored properly (that is, flat) it should remain that way. If a print has been in a tube it is going to be more difficult to frame until it is flat. (This is discussed in the chapter on mounting, page 61. You'll also read here what to do with minor rips and wrinkles; however, if this advice is unsatisfactory, you'll have to employ the spray glue method.)

Frame: The type of frame will be determined by the type of print you are framing.

sentimentally
valuable pieces

Follow a conservation type pattern (see page 169) for the framing, matting, and mounting if you want longevity. Utilize ultraviolet-filter acrylic and rag board.

temple rubbings

Glass: If the temple rubbing is done on a black background, your best bet is nonglare glass. Acrylic and regular glass give a mirrored effect due to the black background. If the temple rubbing is done on a lighter paper, you can use regular glass or acrylic.

Mats and liners: These usually are not called for in framing a temple rubbing.

Mounting: Any temple rubbing smaller than 14″×18″ can be dry mounted with pressure-sensitive dry-mounting tissue used for photos. If it is larger than that, we do not recommend mounting. Use a rag board for backing (since this is probably a sentimentally valuable piece).

Frame: Most temple rubbings are done on a black background with gold wax. We recommend a bright gold frame with a rounded top. For any other background, a narrow gold, black, or wooden-finished frame is effective. We stay away from anything too ornate.

three-dimensional objects

These may include coins, arrowheads, awards, medals, and seashells.

Glass: The type of glass should be regular or acrylic. The objects will have to be in a shadow-box frame and so will be set way back from the glass. Nonglare would make it appear fuzzy.

A treasure from the sea. A great object for a three-dimensional or shadowbox frame. The back and sides are of cocoa-colored suede and the frame is a weathered wood frame, reminiscent of driftwood.

97

Mat: In a three-dimensional frame the background and sides of the frame will be covered with material. Velvets, burlap, suede, silk, and linen are all good materials for this frame. You could also use a liner instead of lining the sides of the three-dimensional frame. It would have to be a tall liner that touched the lip of the frame or glass and angled down to the background. It would also be covered in the same material as the background.

Mounting: There are two types of mounting generally used in three-dimensional framing. If possible you can glue down the object using a silicone glue. You may also wire down the object. Use wire or thick thread that is close in color to the object being framed. Place the holes for the wire or thread so they will not be seen, and glue the object carefully so the glue is not seen. Be sure the object does not protrude beyond the lip of the frame, or the glass will not fit. If you have a tall object you may not be able to use glass. If you don't use glass, you may need to clean the three-dimensional frame from time to time by using a blow hair dryer.

Frame: The frame must be deep enough so the object will not protrude above the lip of the frame. Most of these frames are called cap frames (since they have a narrow top and deep sides).

watercolors

Glass: Regular glass and acrylic are the most desirable. Use an ultraviolet-filter acrylic if you want longevity of the colors. Nonglare would destroy the subtlety of a watercolor.

Mat: On most watercolors a 3″ mat is used. An inner mat of ¼″ or ⅛″ can be added. If a conservation effect is wanted, use only rag board.

Mounting: The watercolor should be hinged at the top of the picture to an all-rag backing. Use regular backing board if you don't want conservation quality.

Frame: When a 3″ mat is used, then a narrow frame is utilized (¼″–1″). A narrow wood frame is usually most tasteful. You could also use a narrow, simple gold-leaf frame.

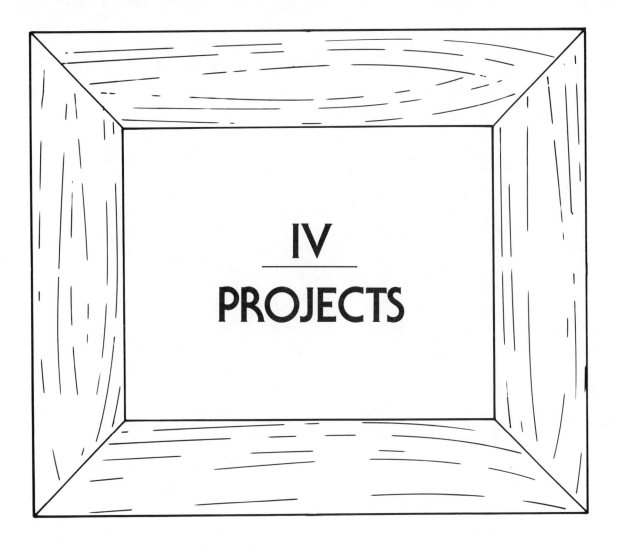

IV
PROJECTS

"barnwood" frame

To BUILD THIS FRAME you need weathered wood. Sources are old houses, weathered barns, fences, and possibly old wood slats from air conditioners found many years ago in the Southwest.

The frame has three parts. Working from the inside out, we start with a ¾'' liner, which you cover with burlap, in keeping with the rustic look. Next, router out a 2½'' wide, ¾'' deep piece of barnwood along the inner edge so the ¾'' liner will fit under it. Saw the outside frame to ¾'' wide and 1⅛'' deep. Don't router out this piece, but cut it, to be nailed to the 2½''-wide panel.

Saw all components to the appropriate width, and then miter to fit one another. Cover the liner using spray glue and then join. Join the other pieces, and then staple the ¾'' liner to the inside of the 2½''wide panel. Place the outer frame around these two pieces so the back of all three pieces lay flat. The outer frame, nailed to the panel, is about ³/₈'' higher in the front. Angle in the nails from the back so they won't show from the sides.

This frame complements any rustic or country art perfectly.

bathroom print

The bathroom or powder room is no longer on the bottom of the decoration list. Depending on your decor, you can use almost any style of artwork in your bath, except for canvas. Steam would most certainly damage canvas and warp the stretcher strips.

The following project is especially appropriate in the bath. A bathtub print with a bright terry cloth mat and a porcelain-looking frame seems the perfect thing for a child's bathroom. The terry towel mat not only coordinates with material used in the bathroom, but also will not be hurt in any way by steam

This print by Julie Corsover Mann becomes a boutique item with a terry towel mat and several coats of white paint on an old frame to give a porcelain look.

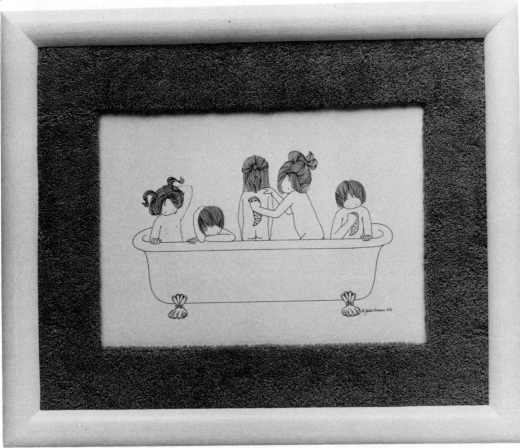

and humidity. This is also a good project on which to try out your mat cutting skills, as the mat will be covered and any minor mistakes you make will not show. For the same reason it's also a good opportunity to use up old mats or odd-colored mat board.

This project is also very economical, since the less-expensive, thin terry cloth towels are easier to work with than thick towels. Use a nice 3″ mat to accentuate the richness of the terry cloth. Follow the instructions for fabric-covered mats on page 44. Glue the fabric mat on the glass. You can use nonglare glass, as it will be right on the print. We bought the frame shown here for $1.00 at a garage sale. At the time it was a ridiculous color and the wrong size! You can convert a similar bargain the way we did. Pull it apart (see page 163), take out the nails, and then cut it to the right size with your miter box. Follow the basic directions for joining the frame back together. Sand the frame smooth and put a few coats of gesso on it, sanding again if necessary. A can of white, glossy spray paint will give it a porcelainlike finish, reminiscent of old-time bathtubs. Fit it all together and you will have a real conversation piece for your bathroom.

bulletin boards

Bulletin boards have always been popular with the younger set and a necessity for all of us with busy schedules. Now that you have developed some new skills in picture framing you can use them for other decorative items like this in your home.

This particular bulletin board was made a little more special by the use of some of these skills. A cork board was covered with fabric spray glued on. A simple wooden frame was painted white with shiny acrylic.

If you don't have an old board you can use, you can order one in a mail-order catalogue. The extra touches you add will make it look like a custom design. If you have a small board you can even cut a paper mat for the inside border of the frame, or use one covered in contrasting fabric.

This bulletin board was from a mail-order
catalogue. It is covered with bright blue linen and
the frame is shiny white.

children's
art gallery

One of the favorite walls in our home, and certainly the one receiving the most comments, is our children's art gallery. While it contains everything from nursery school scribblings to a teen-ager's watercolor, each piece is special to us and deserves special attention. These pictures need only be simply framed to give the most attention to the picture itself.

On some we used old frames repainted to match the pictures along with brightly colored mats. On the pastels we put custom frames—some gold-leaf—with fabric mats and double mats. You can mix in the simply framed with the fancier ones. An acrylic frame with a colored mat is another choice. You can change the picture in this from time to time as the children bring home new "goodies."

Choose the style you want and then follow the directions in our basic instructions (page 27). You can make this spot one that everyone in the house will be proud of. It sure beats using the refrigerator door.

diplomas

We work so hard to get them that we love to show them off. We are talking about diplomas! Don't fall into the trap of the classic black-and-gold frame bought ready-made and mass-produced.

There are an endless variety of things you can do with such a precious piece of paper. Make sure if it is a sheepskin (the majority won't be) that you follow the instructions for conservation mounting (see page 177).

The glass mat (see page 129) treatment is a special one that works well in this case. You can mount the diploma on a small piece of mat in the school color, and can cut a second mat to fit the inside dimensions of the frame in the same color or in the other school color if you wish. Make it very narrow, as the glass mat will be the main feature of this picture. It makes a very special graduation gift for a special person. Use small paper or linen hinges to mount the diploma on the mat board.

If you want to have a more traditional look you can still use the school colors (if they are appropriate) and a gold-leaf frame without the glass mat.

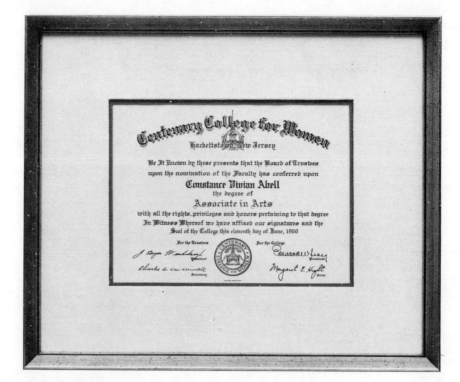

This conservation-mounted sheepskin has an off-white linen mat with a small gray inner mat. An antique gold-leaf frame is one option for framing diplomas.

easels

Any picture sitting on a table, étagère, or bookcase will be greatly enhanced by the addition of a custom-made easel. This makes the picture as attractive from the back as it is from the front. The first easel described here is made up of a fabric-covered back for the frame and a fabric-covered stand to prop the picture up. The back and stand are both made up of cardboard, grayboard, or mat board. The possibilities for fabric coverings are endless; suede, cotton, velvet, silk, linen, and design fabric are all suitable. The second easel presented here is made of acrylic. It's easy to do and unobtrusive.

FABRIC-COVERED EASEL

EASEL BACK

Cut a piece of cardboard, grayboard, or mat board so that its outside dimensions are $1/16''$ smaller than the outside dimensions of the frame for which you're creating the easel. (That way, when the cardboard has been covered with fabric it won't stick out beyond the edge of the frame.)

Cut a piece of fabric about $1/2''$ larger all around than the easel back. Spray glue one side of the cardboard easel back, as well as the wrong side of the fabric. When the glue becomes sticky, center the cardboard on the fabric, glued sides together.

Trim the corners of the fabric as shown in Step 1.   Spray glue the edges of the fabric again, wait until they're tacky, then wrap around the cardboard as shown in Step 2.

EASEL STAND

Cut an easel stand in the shape shown in Step 2. It should be almost as high as the easel back, and approximately one-third as wide at the bottom. Place a horizontal crease in the stand $1/2''$-$3/4''$ from the top. (This is where you'll be bending the stand in order to glue the top of it to the easel back.)

Cut two pieces of fabric for the easel stand; one should be the same shape but slightly smaller than the stand. The other should be cut as shown in Step 3.

A table full of small pictures is a focal point in the
living room or bedroom. Here are fabric frames
with fabric easels and regular frames on brass and
wooden easels. It's fun to add to the collection and
have a variety of types.

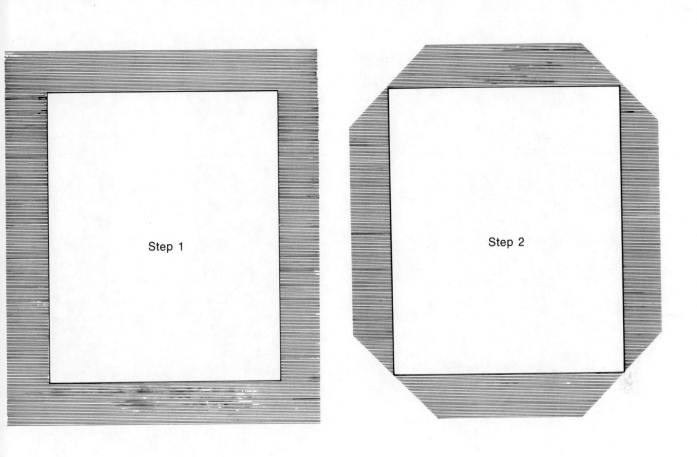

Step 1

Step 2

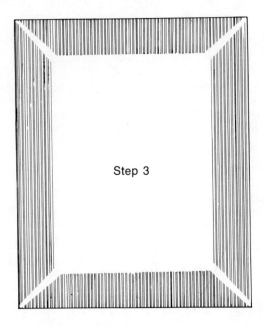

Step 3

Covering back of easel with fabric.

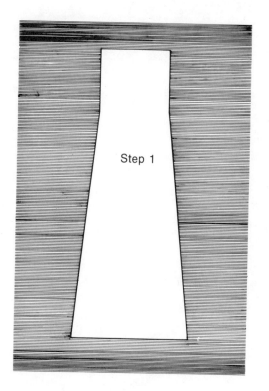

Step 1

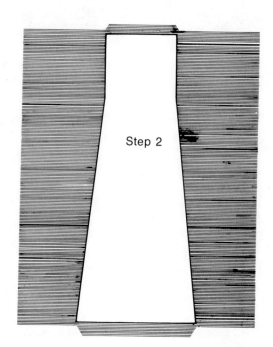

Step 2

Step 3

Covering easel stand with fabric.

First, spray glue the wrong side of the smaller piece of fabric. When the glue is tacky, lay the cardboard stand on top of it with what will be its underside facing down. Turn over and smooth out the fabric.

Now spray glue the larger piece of fabric. Lay the stand, cloth-covered side *up*, on the fabric. Let dry a few minutes. Spray the fabric edges again, and when they are tacky fold them over the easel back as shown: first the sides, then the top and bottom. Smooth out and let dry.

STRAP

Next you need a strap, $1/2''$-$5/8''$ wide and long enough to reach from stand to cover, in order to keep the stand from collapsing. Cut a piece of fabric roughly $1''$ wide, and about as long as your frame is wide. Spray glue the wrong side of the fabric. When it gets tacky, fold it in half lengthwise to make a tube. Lay the tube on the table with the seam side up; flatten the strap with your hand, keeping the seam in the center of the strap. (The seam will face down when installed, and won't show.)

Now pull the seam apart for a length of $3/4''$ at one end of the strap. Slit it on either side so that it opens into a rectangle as in Step 3. Trim the rectangle to a small size.

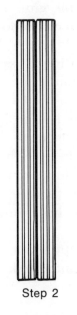

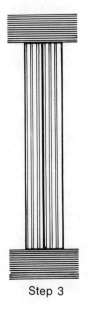

Step 1 Step 2 Step 3

Tension strap for easel.

115

ASSEMBLY

To attach the strap to the easel stand, five-minute epoxy is best to use. (It has many uses around the house and is well worth the purchase.) Mix the two parts of it together in equal amounts as the instructions specify. Using a wooden stick (a putty stick or popsicle stick will do) apply the epoxy to the underside of the square, then attach the square near the bottom of the easel stand, being sure to center it along the width. Now sandwich the strap and easel stand between two pieces of cardboard (so you won't dent the fabric) and clamp it with a C clamp or spring clamp for five minutes to dry.

Now, with a single-edge razor, cut a slit in the easel back for the strap. Make it as wide as the strap, and as high up from the bottom of the easel back as it is on the easel stand. Take a screwdriver and push the end of the strap through the slit until you can reach it with your fingers and pull it through farther. Don't adjust the length yet.

Now mix some more epoxy, and apply to the top back of the easel stand. Attach the stand in the center of the easel back near the top. When it has dried, adjust the length of the strap so that the angle of the stand is correct. If the easel is to go on a low table, it should be at a 65° angle; 75° if on a high shelf. Lean your frame against the easel back to be sure you've got the angle you want.

Take the end of the strap sticking through the easel back and pull that end apart to form a rectangle as you did the other. Glue it down and tape it to the easel back. (The tape will hold the strap in place until the glue dries.) Now you have a complete easel and all you have to do is attach it to the frame.

These are two ways to attach the easel to the frame: with contact cement, or by using brass tacks with rounded heads. We prefer the contact cement because the brass tacks are too obtrusive when seen from the back. Contact cement has to be used in a well-ventilated area. It must be applied to both surfaces—the back of the frame and the reverse side of the easel back—$1/8''$ to $1/4''$ in from the outer edge. Apply a small, thin band of it $1/4''$ in width around the perimeter of the two surfaces. Follow the directions for using the cement very carefully; do not try to rush the drying time or you may ruin the project.

If you choose to use the brass tacks, hammer them through the fabric-covered back into the frame $2''$-$3''$ apart all the way around.

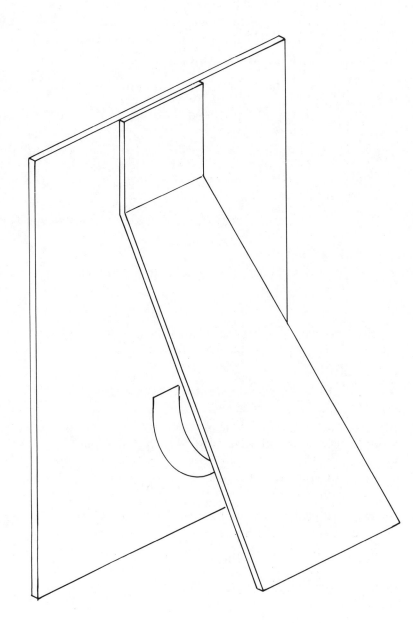

Completed easel.

ACRYLIC EASEL

An acrylic easel stand consists of two narrow L-shaped strips of acrylic that are fastened to the lower back corners of your picture frame. When you use an acrylic easel, be sure to cover the back of the frame with an extra special dust cover. Decorator fabric or fancy paper would be nice.

The first step is to cut your two acrylic strips. They shouldn't show from the front of the frame, so cut them narrower than the width of the moulding. If the moulding measures $3/4''$ in width, make the acrylic $1/2''$ wide. Use the following guide to determine the length and thickness of the acrylic strip.

Frame	Acrylic	
	Length	Thickness
$8'' \times 10''$	$6''$	$1/8''$
$12'' \times 16''$	$8''$	$1/8''$
$16'' \times 20''$	$8''$	$1/4''$

Set the iron on a cotton setting and let it heat up fully. Grasp one end of the acrylic strip in each hand, and hold the center of it about $1/8''$ away from the outer edge of the iron. In a few minutes the acrylic should feel like it is starting to flex in your hands. Wait a few seconds longer so the acrylic will be pliable, take it away from the iron and bend to an appropriate angle—65° if the picture will set on a low table, 75° if on a high shelf. Be sure to use a protractor to measure the angle. Do not worry about touching the protractor to the acrylic; the acrylic is pliable, but not melted.

Bend the other acrylic strip in the same fashion, measuring it against the first acrylic stand to be sure they are at the same angle. If you have trouble matching the angle, merely reheat the acrylic and adjust.

There are two methods that can be used to attach the acrylic stand to the picture frame.

1. Two pan head screws can be placed in each piece of acrylic. Drill holes through the acrylic and into the frame. In the acrylic, the holes should be the size of the screw and in the back of the frame they should be a tad smaller for a tight fit.

2. The second method is to use five-minute epoxy, which gives a much neater, finished look.

Lay the framed picture face down on the table. Hold one of the acrylic stands in final position on the frame, and determine how much of the length you can trim off it to make it less visi-

ble. If the bend in the acrylic is slightly off center, you can now trim the strip to put it in the middle. For instance, a 6″ strip can be trimmed to have 2¼″ on either side of the bend.

Now position the stands on the frame where you want them to be and outline them with pencil. (If you position the frame ¼″-³/₈″ up on the acrylic stand, it will give the appearance of floating.) Make indentations ⅛″-³/₁₆″ deep along the pencil marks with an ice pick or nail.

Mix epoxy, and use a putty stick to spread it on the side of the acrylic that will be attached to the frame. Also put epoxy along the indentations you've made on the back of the frame, letting it sink in. This will help support the weight of the picture; because the indentations break through the dust cover, the glue will be absorbed into something more solid than paper or fabric.

Now mount the acrylic stands and let dry. Your project is finished, leaving you with something both functional and extra attractive.

ethiopian scroll

This scroll was about a thousand years old and had been written on goatskin. We wanted to protect it for future generations and still show it off. The owners knew it would be hanging in a sunlit room, so special ultraviolet-filter acrylic was used to prevent rapid fading. Other special precautions had to be taken. Any time you are framing an antiquity there will be different features and different needs. We will touch on some of the details of this one.

Because the scroll was written on skin it could not be permanently mounted. To keep the scroll in place we used acrylic brackets. We purchased one acrylic sheet approximately 8"×10" and trimmed eight pieces 1/4"×3" with an acrylic cutter. We used a heating element, which can be purchased at any store specializing in acrylics (an iron would have worked as well), to bend the acrylic into two 90° angles so that it made a square S shape. We then made slits in the linen-covered rag board on which we were mounting the scroll, slipped one end of each bracket into a slit, and glued them to the back of the linen mat to hold them stationary.

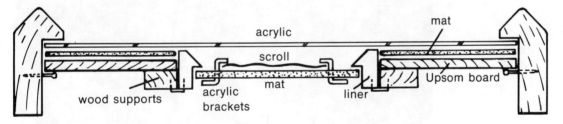

Cross section

acrylic

mat

scroll

mat

Upsom board

wood supports

acrylic brackets

liner

When all the acrylic brackets were glued in we were ready to install the scroll. Three tiny stitches were sewn on the top of the scroll to hold it to the linen-covered rag board. Colored thread coordinated with the linen or skin kept the thread invisible. Two tiny stitches held the bottom loosely in place. These bottom stitches also kept the scroll from curling up and touching the acrylic.

A deep antique gold frame was used, with an inner liner to hold the glass off the scroll. A wide mat of linen coordinated with the linen background.

Simplicity yet elegance are important so as not to detract from the art piece. And a double purpose has been served here: The antiquity will be preserved for some time to come, while it is enjoyable now, for all to view.

Special acrylic brackets were designed to keep this thousand-year-old Ethiopian scroll in place without destroying it. A gold leaf frame and vanilla-colored linen are additional special effects that highlight this beautiful heirloom. Ultra-violet filtered plexiglass will help keep the elements away from the scroll.

fabric frames

Fabric frames are fun to make and a handsome addition to your decor. If you've ever checked in a boutique or gift shop you will see that fabric frames are very expensive; making them yourself is both easy and economical.

As an easy project, take an old frame with simple lines, spray glue it, and cover it with fabric. This is a great way to hide an old, scratched moulding.

The fabric frame shown is easier to make than it looks. It is simply a mat covered with fabric. For the three-dimensional effect a ¼''-thick polyester foam is used to cover the mat, and then the fabric is applied. Use the mat-cutting techniques found in this book and then the mat-covering directions. For the finishing touch follow the directions for the easel back.

family picture gallery

Today all ages are interested in their "roots." Our recent acquisition of a large box of old family photos proved that our family was no exception. A family gallery was the end result. The subject matter ranged from a 125-year-old photo of a great-great grandmother to our family today. Each picture is framed according to the time and style it represents. You can start with one or two pictures and build your gallery over a period of time. Don't feel that you must have a wall full of photos to start your gallery. Half the fun is watching it grow.

We do have some nice new frames in the gallery, but many of the frames are old, antique, refurbished, and combinations of old mats used with new frames. Mats of long ago are beautiful and unique, and whenever possible we like to use them. One of the most unusual pictures in the group has its original 65-year-old mat and an old frame covered in oatmeal-colored linen. Mingled in with these lovely old photos are pictures of our children taken last year.

As with any grouping you can add pictures as you inherit more and as time permits their framing. It will be a family fun project for one and all.

An oil painting on canvas by Texas artist Oris Robertson is simply framed in a floater frame so as not to detract from the beauty of the painting.

floater frames

The floater frame got its name because it gives the appearance that the artwork is floating within the frame. A stretched canvas is very successfully framed this way. The moulding employed here is sometimes called a step moulding because of its shape observed from an end view.

When measuring the canvas, measure *both* sides of the length and *both* sides of the width because a stretched canvas is often out of square. The largest side of the width and the largest side of the length will determine the size of the moulding. If each piece of moulding is cut to fit the canvas it would also be out of square and would be noticeable to the eye. However, with the frame in square, it minimizes the visual awareness of the out-of-square canvas, making it less obvious.

Measure the moulding from the bottom step, since this is where the stretcher strips of the canvas will rest.

If the canvas is larger on one length by ¼″ or more, a different type of frame should be chosen. Pick a frame that has a large lip to make up the difference. Or else restretch the canvas in square.

When a canvas is stretched, the staples are sometimes placed on the side of the canvas. These are obvious to the viewer observing the art from a slight angle. To alleviate this the edge of the canvas can be painted black or a coordinating color. Be very careful if you paint and *do not use masking tape as a guide,* as it could pull off some of the artwork.

A safer way to cover the staples is to utilize black electrician's tape. Do not stretch the tape, as it would eventually fall off.

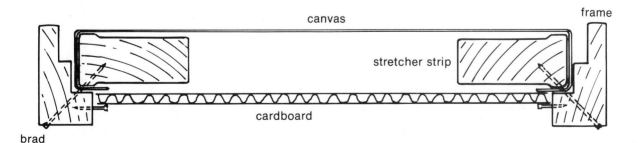

brad / canvas / frame / stretcher strip / cardboard

Note the illustration for the placement of brads in the frame to hold the canvas to the frame. The nailholes should be pre-drilled with a slightly smaller drill bit. Note how the cardboard was placed in the frame to protect the canvas from punctures from the back. This also keeps bugs out of the back of the picture.

glass mats

When a picture is mounted between two pieces of glass with an appropriate amount of glass showing around the picture it gives the effect of floating. To get a double floating effect, you can use a deep frame so that the picture appears to be floating away from the wall as well.

This high school diploma is floating between two pieces of glass and has a French line made with architectural tape.

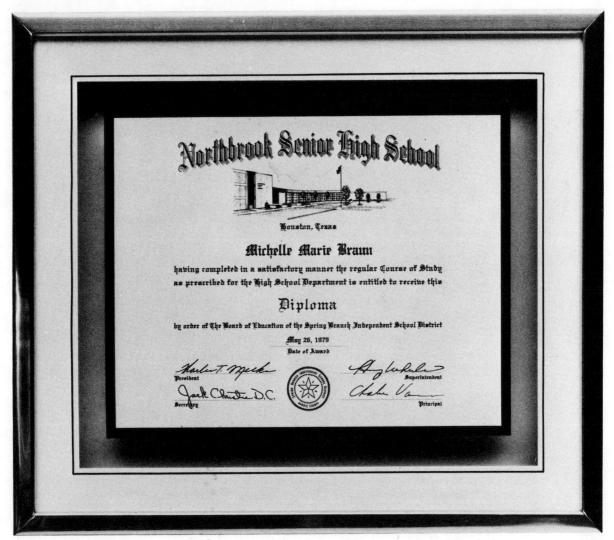

While glass mats offer an eclectic and interesting alternative to more conventional mats, there are other reasons for using two pieces of glass. Sometimes there is something on the back of the picture that needs to be seen either for historical or factual value. If the style of the picture or your decor would not lend itself to a glass mat, you could opt to use a paper or cloth mat and still use a piece of glass or acrylic on the back so you may view and still protect any factual information.

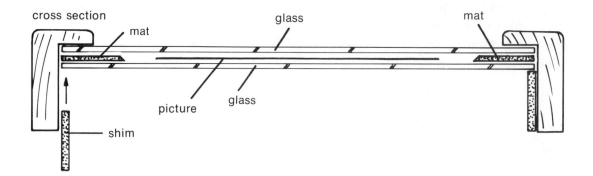

cross section   mat   glass   mat
picture   glass
shim

The picture will be heavier with two pieces of glass, so you must take extra precautions to make the frame strong enough to support the extra weight. Follow basic instructions for joining the frame, but leave the frame in the vise for a full ten minutes. This will ensure that the glue dries sufficiently. After gluing the corners, join them with a minimum of three nails per corner. Install two on the easier side to nail and one on the harder side. If the frame is deep you can even use four nails—two on each side. Never use just one nail, as it would act as an axis.

For added protection you can use acrylic instead of glass. Acrylic has several advantages over glass. Acrylic is light in weight, which is an especially big factor if you have a large picture. Furthermore, it's not so susceptible to condensation because it is a thermal insulator and does not change temperature as fast as glass.

Be very exact in measuring and cutting the glass so you can fit the glass into the frame easily. The less gap between the frame and glass, the less problem you will have fitting the picture.

You can use different-size borders, ranging from 1¼'' to 8''. Remember, the wider the glass mat the greater the floating effect, and the more startling it will appear.

If the picture is mounted you are ready to go. Clean the glass and then attach the back of the mounted picture to the back of the glass with little dabs of white glue or a silicone glue. Allow it to dry for one hour. If you have two-faced tape you can put some on the back of the mounted picture to help hold it while the glue dries. You may need to clean the glass some more after the gluing process is done. The top piece of clean glass or acrylic can act as a weight while the glue is drying. You can now paint the inside of the frame black if you're planning to use nails to hold the glass in the frame (this is the easiest way). Black acts as a shadow. Or you can paint the four sides the color of the frame.

If the picture is unmounted you can attach it to a piece of noncorrugated cardboard such as mat or illustration board. Never mount the picture itself directly to the glass. Do not use Scotch tape or masking tape to mount since they contain acidic qualities that would bleed through the picture in months. There are two types of usable adhesives that are readily available. The first, dry-mount tissue, can be obtained at a photo shop. Cut long, thin strips (for example, $1/2''$x$3''$), preferably two, one for each side of the top edge of the picture. Lay the tissue on top of the cardboard, lay the picture on top of that, then use a clean piece of paper such as typing paper for your cover sheet. Place that over the print, center the picture on the cardboard, and place a weight on the picture so it does not move.

Heat up the iron until it reaches a temperature that will melt dry-mount tissue (low heat, about 200°). You can experiment with a scrap before trying this on the picture.

Run the tip of the iron over the cover sheet where the dry-mount tissue is stationed. Remember that the two pieces are placed at the top of the picture, so it hangs from the top. This will allow it to move as the changing environment may cause it to do. If you anchor the bottom, the picture could ripple and wrinkle. You cannot mount photos with this method. Photos should be dry-mounted with one of the new pressure sensitive adhesive sheets. A good one is made by 3M.

In the second method, use an adhesive tape—bookbinders' or linen tape. You can even use gummed reinforcements for notebook paper on small pictures. Cut off an appropriate length of tape (for example, a $16''\times20''$ picture would require two strips), each one about $1''\times2''$. Fold them in half to $1/2''\times2''$. Brush water on one side of the gummed tape, and place that half on top of the cardboard. After that dries, do the same thing to the other side, being sure not to use too much water, as it will bleed through, especially if the picture is thin. Center the picture on top of the glass with glue as previously explained, placing the top piece of glass on the picture to act as a weight. Let the glue dry for at least two hours before you try to assemble everything.

Take a whisk broom and sweep all the dust away from the work area and from inside your frame. Lay the frame face down on the table. Place a book (you may need more than one, depending on the size of the frame) in the center of the frame and place the glass-matted picture on top of the book. This will elevate the glass over the frame. Lift the frame up to envelop the glass mat, then use the frame with the glass mat safely inside to push the book out of the way, and lay the whole thing back down on the table.

If you choose to use nails in the frame, take care not to hit the glass. Use small, thin brads, place them 2''–3'' apart, and then clip the brads so they will not show from the front.

If your frame is larger than 14''×18'' you will need to use shims instead of nails to hold the glass or acrylic in the frame. A shim is a long, thin strip of wood, cardboard, or acrylic that will be glued on the inside of the frame to secure the acrylic or glass in the frame. Choose the material you will use and cut the shims so they will fit snugly inside the frame from one end to the other. A good time to cut these is while the glue is drying on the glass. If you are using shims you can paint them as you would the inside of the frame. You can match them to the frame or paint them dark gray, which gives the illusion of a shadow.

To affix the shims to the frame, use two-faced tape and white glue. If the shim is wide enough you can put strips of glue and tape side by side; otherwise alternate them. The tape will hold the shims in place until the glue dries. If you don't have any two-faced tape, then use spring clamps or C clamps to hold until the glue dries. Allow two hours before attempting to move the picture. To hang, install two sawtooth hangers or mirror hangers.

greeting cards

Have you ever seen greeting cards that you thought were lovely enough to use as art pieces? It is easy today to find cards with no words on the outside: the stores are full of them and they make a marvelous and inexpensive addition to any grouping. A series of reproductions of works of old masters and famous artists can be found in many stationery and card stores. Small ones look nice on an easel on a table or bookcase, or hung on a wall just above a small table.

They are framed as you would any small print. A mat can be used (paper or fabric) and any appropriate frame. What nicer gift than to frame a card and return it to the sender?

An oval-cut paper mat covered with the fabric used to cover the wall makes this mirror special. The frame is a mirror also.

mirror

"Mirror, mirror, on the wall—who's the fairest of them all?" In this case the mirror itself could win a prize. A mirror can be a candidate for your framing talents just as any picture would.

A fabric mat and a discarded frame that we fixed up turned this mirror into a daughter's delight. There are many variations that can be used on mirrors. An oval was cut as on page 40 and covered with fabric to match the curtains and bedspread. The wood was painted to match the room also. You can use any moulding you choose. The mat and mirror are fitted into the frame just as a picture would be.

136 *Top: The needlepoint Tiger Lily is simply framed with a small green frame. Bottom: At a later date a liner covered with yellow linen and a shiny green metal frame is added. The original frame becomes the inner liner. Many simple frames can be used as liners.*

needlepoint
and crewelwork

The possibilities for framing your needlework are endless, but there are a few guidelines to follow. While you needn't have a mat or a liner, the addition of one can only enhance the picture. A paper mat is really a no-no. It is flat and does not complement the texture of the needlework. Linen, cotton, and velvet are all suitable fabrics.

Deciding whether to use glass is a major consideration. While the piece is more attractive without glass, the glass is a definite protection over the years. Do not substitute acrylic, as it contains static electricity and you would constantly be fighting dust and fabric fibers. You will need to use regular glass if the needlework is highly textured or has thick stitches. This is a good time to utilize a fabric-covered liner between the needlework and the frame. This way the glass will not squash the texture effect. If the glass will be right next to the needlework you can use nonglare glass. If you don't use glass, you should use a fabric spray protector.

MEASURING NEEDLEWORK

The needlework will be stretched over a piece of Upsom board or $3/16''$ cardboard. You must determine its measurements so you can cut the backing board.

Measuring needlepoint is not as difficult as for crewelwork because the canvas that the needlepoint is stitched on must not show; thus the outside perimeter of the needlepoint stitches will be the measuring guide. Place the ruler at one end of the stitches, pinch the needlepoint and ruler together, and pull the needlepoint taut. First measure that side; then do the same to the side parallel to it. Be sure to measure all four sides, because needlepoint will quite often be stitched slightly out of square. If one is $16''$ and one is $16^1/4''$, compromise and cut that length of Upsom board $16^1/8''$.

Measuring a needlepoint

Mounting a needlepoint

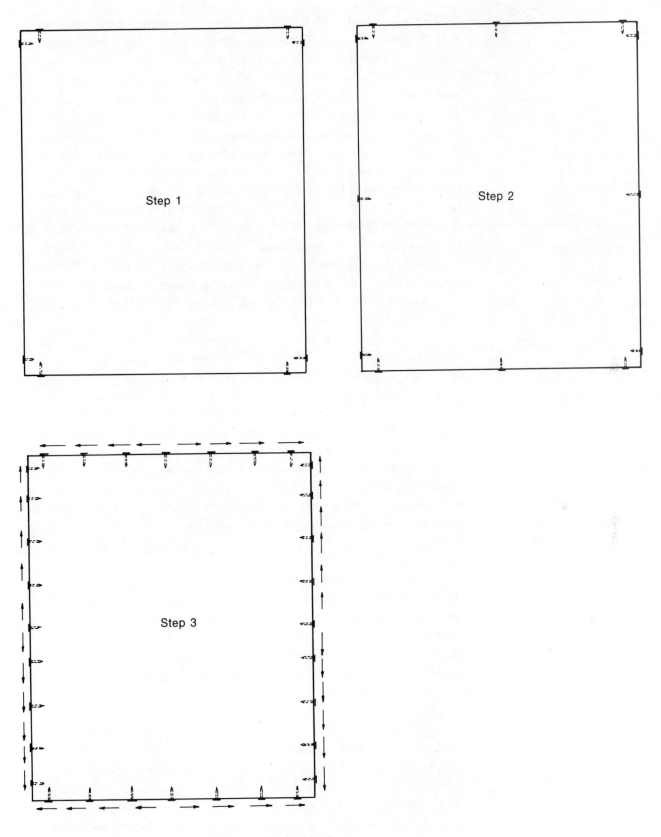

Tack placement. Arrows show direction of tack placement.

In some needlework there is excess stitching on the reverse side that is extremely bulky and shows up as ridges and lumps from the front side. Padding the Upsom board will solve this problem. You can use three types of padding: felt, 1/8'' or 1/4'' foam rubber, or quilting batting. Felt is the most accessible and easiest to use. White felt should be your first choice because it is less acidic than colored felt. The foam rubber is spongier and will give the needlework a rich, puffy, almost three-dimensional effect. It does contain acid but shouldn't harm the picture for at least a couple of decades. Quilting batting is very thick, and thin layers must be pulled off. If you desire a three-dimensional effect, you can pull off thicker layers. It is not very acidic and is a good choice when you want to pass down something from one generation to another. If you are not going to use padding, you can place a sheet of 100% acid-free rag between the Upsom board and needlework to increase the longevity of the piece.

Cut the Upsom board to the desired measurement and then glue the padding on the board. If you use spray glue, first overcut the padding, then spray glue one side of the Upsom board.

Crewelwork has little corner marks that are used as a guideline when you measure and stretch. Place the measuring tape or ruler on one of the corner marks and, pinching the ruler and needlework together at that point, pull the crewelwork tight to see where the other corner measurement lands. Be sure not to pull so tightly that the stitches start to separate. After measuring the length and width of the crewelwork, cut the Upsom board to those dimensions, using a straight edge and spring clamp and a utility knife.

Some crewelwork has a decorated border that needs to show within the frame. This type of crewelwork usually will not have corner marks, so you will need to make your own. Use a pencil (that way you can erase any marks that are wrong) and place rows of marks about 1'' apart on all four sides. Place the marks 1/2''–3'' away from the border. If the piece has a small border or a plain border you can leave a wider margin of fabric.

Spray glue one side of the Upsom board. Allow the glue to get tacky and sticky, about two to five minutes, then lay the Upsom board on top of the padding and trim off the excess with a single-edge razor blade, utility knife, or scissors.

If you want to use white glue, make an X of glue across the Upsom board. Next make a thin line of glue around the perimeter about 1/2''–1'' in from the outside edge. Lay the padding on top and allow to dry for two hours, then trim with a utility knife or a pair of scissors.

Now you are ready to stretch and mount the needlework. First anchor each corner of your piece to the respective corner of Upsom board, using corner marks for the crewelwork and the edge stitches on the needlework. Use either a staple gun or a hammer and tacks. After anchoring each corner move to the center of the sides and anchor them. Start in the center of one side, then in the center of the side that is parallel to that side. Proceed in this manner until the whole needlework is tacked down. As you approach the corners you may notice a slight ripple in the fabric. This can be easily removed by tugging and pulling until it is gone. Stretching pliers that are commonly used in stretching artist canvas can be of help here. You can remove the corner tacks and work the wrinkle out, then rean-chor the corner. Keep an eye on the lines in the stitches and the overall squareness of the needlework.

When you finish mounting the needlework you can wrap the excess material around the back of the board and tack it down. Be sure the tacks or staples do not go through to the front. Trim if necessary. You are now ready to frame.

Mat-cutting how-to for the home framer

IF A PICTURE is worth a thousand words, the mat used to surround the artwork undoubtedly deserves mention. In correct proportion and an enhancing color, a mat flatters both picture and frame.

Determined doers learned about buying readymade frames long ago, but the mat-cutting process often puts off even the most resourceful. The technique is more clear cut when outlined by a professional.

One of the big hurdles for the amateur mat cutter has always been equipment, according to picture framer Sherwood McCall of Houston. A mat cut with a razor or similar blade is haphazard, and professional equipment is prohibitively expensive.

However, there are mat cutters that sell for less than $10 and are perfectly adequate, says McCall. "I use one of those and a 24-inch metal T-square for most of the mat sizes I need.

"Ask for mat board at any art store. It comes in about 60 or 70 colors, and a sheet that measures about 30 by 40 inches sells for around $2," he adds.

TO DETERMINE mat size for any given picture, first measure the size of the artwork and decide on the dimensions of the frame. The perimeter of the mat will fit the inside dimensions of the frame or what framers call the "rabbit."

The "rabbit" is the lip or small ledge on which rest the glass, mat, artwork, and backing board that when layered together complete the framed picture.

"I use about a half-inch more mat on the bottom of a large picture than I do around the other sides. Most professional framers do because after you hang a picture, there's an optical illusion: The bottom of the mat looks smaller than it really is.

"Making the mat larger on the bottom than on the other sides is much more effective on a vertical picture, though, than on a horizontal one; sometimes it looks funny on a horizontal."

ONCE the dimensions of the mat are determined, cut mat board to size so that it fits into frame. Make cuts on reverse side of mat board to avoid marring the part that will show.

Then you're ready to make pencil marks to be used as cutting guidelines on the reverse side of the mat. Use T-square to make sure lines are straight and perpendicular to each other and mat edges.

"When making marks, you should end up with a tic-tac-toe pattern of four pencil lines extending all the way from one

In the picture framing business for nine years, Sherwood McCall gives mat-cutting demonstrations.

side of mat to the other, from top to bottom," explains McCall. "The inside square will be the opening in the mat when you've finished cutting."

BEFORE CUTTING, make sure the mat cutter blade protrudes just enough to cut through the mat. Place blade next to mat edge to see if blade is out too far; if so, it will make cutting more difficult because two surfaces instead of one will have to be penetrated by the blade.

Use a scrap of mat board for cutting surface. Don't cut on glass, steel, or other hard surfaces that dull mat cutter blade.

Once mat cutter blade is adjusted, make first cut by beginning at inside lower left corner of pencil markings. Align face of mat cutter with pencil guidelines; then insert blade in mat where pencil lines intersect.

Align T-square or straight edge with pencil lines, and use it as guide to slide mat cutter away from body toward top left corner of mat board to point where pencil lines meet.

"I USE about the weight of my arm and then a little bit more downward pressure," explains McCall. "Follow the same procedure on other side of mat board, turning board clockwise as you work."

A few practice sessions with scrap board are suggested by McCall, who adds that four or five tries should do it.

Once practiced, the amateur mat cutter can go on to more advanced techniques such as cutting double or multiple mats.

Nancy Adams

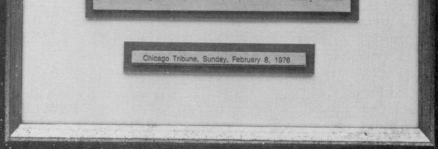

Chicago Tribune, Sunday, February 8, 1976

newspaper clippings

They wrinkle, tear, and yellow with age unless protected—so what better way to do this than to frame your important newspaper clippings? A wedding, graduation, promotion, or any important occasion can be preserved for posterity in this way.

When framing a news clipping you will usually find in measuring that it is out of square; if so, you should mat it. But instead of the standard procedure you will need to mount the clipping on a black mat with spray glue. This will keep the writing on the reverse side from showing through. Then trim the article and mat so it will be as even as possible. The other alternative is to trim the article first and then mount on the black mat. Trim the mat so 1/8'' shows all the way around the

Trimming a 1/8'' mat around a newspaper clipping

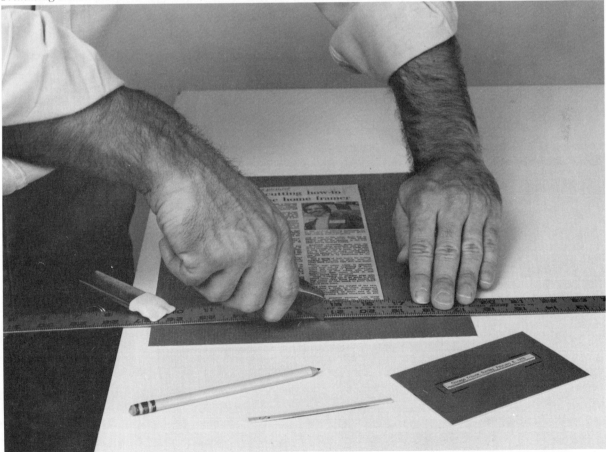

article. This highlights the article. As a little extra feature you can mount the name of the paper and the date in the same fashion and center it under the article. When trimming newspaper you can use either scissors or a utility knife. If you use the knife make sure you hold the blade at a 60° angle to keep the paper from ripping. For ease in trimming the mat you can make it larger and then trim it to ⅛" after you have glued the article on it.

The mounted article is now mounted on a mat cut to fit the inside dimensions of your frame. A lighter shade works well with the newsprint and the black border. A medium-gray mat and a simple silver-leaf antique frame tie it all together. Regular or nonglare glass can be used. You are not limited to gray and black, although these work well. We framed an article about an alumnus and his college and used the school colors, blue and gray. This worked very well and tied in with the story.

If the quality of your clipping is poor you can usually order a photo copy from the newspaper for a fee. It will be of a higher quality than the original. It is a very special way to congratulate someone for his or her special happening.

pencil or pen-and-ink drawings

If there is an aspiring artist in your family, you are sure to have some pencil sketches around. When framed attractively, they make welcome additions to your decor and art collection. Our favorite treatment is to use two shades of gray for a double-beveled mat. If you desire more color you can certainly use it, but a bright, bold color would dominate the picture and be inappropriate. Metal contemporary and aluminum frames go well with these pictures.

Our picture called for an antique frame to coordinate with the feeling that an old house portrayed.

If the artist has signed it and/or numbered it, be certain to let this show when framing it. Who knows? Maybe someday your artist will be famous!

photo frames that are inexpensive

If you love family snapshots as much as we do, it would be impossible to custom-frame all of them. The cost would be prohibitive. But this simple procedure can allow you the look of a custom-frame job while holding down the cost.

Old dime-store gold frames are used and the plastic inner liner is covered with fabric. The job is done with spray glue, it takes only minutes, and the change is miraculous. If the frame is the narrow gold type with no inner liner you have several options. You can use the frame as a liner and put a wooden moulding around it. This enlarges it and makes it a little fancier. A second option is to cover the entire metal frame (or old wooden one) with some fabric. Again, a simple spray-glue job. You can also take some narrow ribbon (such as velvet) and glue it on the metal frame.

Since these dime-store frames come with an easel back, you can make it a little more special by covering the easel with the same fabric. They will look sensational on a table or in a bookcase. Mix in some plants, some books, and you have a focal point in the room. Application of these ideas takes little time and money and you will be pleased with the results.

Here are several ideas for framing posters. Some are used in children's rooms and are simply framed. Others have mats and glass and are treated as artwork.

posters

The popularity of posters knows no age boundary, and everyone in our family has posters. Normally they wrinkle and tear and their life expectancy is rather short, but you can take certain steps to prolong it. Posters are marvelous in decorating bare walls, and can be some of the simplest and most inexpensive objects to frame.

A Degas poster mounted on foam-core and framed with braquettes. Back view of poster framed with braquettes.

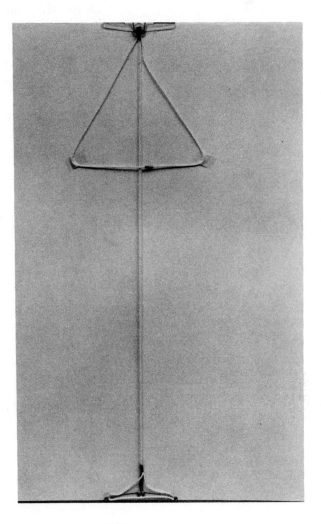

The kitten for a teen-age girl's room was simply spray glued on a piece of foam core or featherweight board. They are readily available at an art store. They are very light in weight, so require only the simplest and narrowest of frames. No glass is used. The football poster is also mounted on foam core, and in this case no frame is used. Four blocks of lattice (thin wooden strips $1/8''$ – $3/16''$ thick) are glued on the back of the foam core, and a sawtooth hanger is used to hang it. What a great way to frame for children who change their rock-group and sports-team allegiances from year to year.

A bit more money and time went into the framing of the next poster; it is treated as a piece of art and hung in a grouping. Nonglare glass was preferred, so only a single mat was chosen. A metal frame that you can put together yourself completes this poster.

Most museums have beautiful posters that can be purchased in their art shop or book store. The cost is reasonable and it can also be a reminder of a memorable time. Such was the case with the Degas poster. We were fortunate to see the Degas showing while in New York and purchased the poster at the Metropolitan Museum of Art. We chose the braquettes for a simple, uncluttered framing look. The ideas are endless, and really anything goes when framing posters. Let your time and pocketbook be your guides, and have fun. You will love the results.

Usually when you purchase a poster or large print it is rolled in a tube. Remove it and store between two pieces of cardboard for a couple of days or until you decide to frame it. It will flatten out and be easier to work with.

FOAM CORE MOUNTED POSTER

TOOLS AND MATERIALS:

foam core board (a plastic foam laminated between two pieces of
   heavyweight paper)
spray glue
glue
four pieces of $1\frac{1}{2}'' \times \frac{1}{8}''$ lattice
sawtooth hangers
brayer
spring clamp
metal straight edge
utility knife

Mount the print on foam core following the instructions for spray-glue mounting (see page 61). Be sure to spray glue both surfaces, as there will be no frame, and the extra sticking power will be needed. After mounting the print on the foam core, the excess foam core must be trimmed away. Attach the metal straight edge with a spring clamp and make sure your knife has a sharp blade. Hold the knife at an extreme angle to the foam core so you get a nice clean cut. There will be no frame to hide any ragged edges. Place the foam core-mounted poster face down on a clean, flat surface and attach the lattice pieces at each corner. Be sure to come in enough from each corner so the lattice will not show. Attach the lattice pieces with white glue. Tape the strips down so they won't move while they dry. Put some heavy books or similar object on the strips for about an hour. This will keep the foam core flat, and once it is flat you will notice that it stays that way. Two sawtooth hangers complete the project. The poster is pleasant to look at (how many ripped ones have you thrown away?) and you have not invested heavily in time or money.

POSTERS WITH A FRAME AND NO GLASS

With a little extra expense you can add a frame. No glass is used, so you can use a thinner, lighter frame, still keeping your cost to a minimum. Follow our previous instructions for mounting. You don't need to be perfect in trimming the foam core, as the edge will be hidden from view by the frame. Follow basic instructions for fitting a picture (without glass). Screw eyes and wire can be used for hanging in this instance.

POSTERS WITH FRAME AND GLASS

This poster is used as an art piece in the home, so you frame the poster as you would a print. The poster is not mounted but is hinged with linen tape onto a piece of cardboard. If you can't find linen tape, use brown gummed tape, which is better than masking tape. A single-mat, nonglare glass and the aluminum frame you buy and put together yourself make this a simple project to assemble.

BRAQUETTES

For our Degas poster we wanted a special effect. The one you get using braquettes (available at art supply stores) is very chic and contemporary. It gives an uncluttered look that mixes well in a grouping.

The poster was not mounted. A piece of foam core was cut to the same outside dimensions as the poster. A utility knife held at an extreme angle to the foam core gives a very clean edge. Be certain that the blade is very sharp. You can get an Arkansas stone at a hardware store and sharpen your own blades. This way you will not need to replace them as often. Be sure to use water instead of oil on the stone when sharpening your blades, as the oil will soil your blade and get on the materials.

Acrylic is best to use with the braquettes, since the edges will be exposed and acrylic is less susceptible to breakage than glass. Acrylic is also lighter than glass. Regular or nonglare glass can be used, but be sure the edges are sanded so they will not be sharp. If you decide to use glass have the glass supplier cut and sand or seam the edges for you.

Place the foam core on a flat, clean surface, then top it with the poster and then the acrylic. The acrylic will come covered on both sides with a protective paper. One side of the paper must be removed before you place it on the poster—an easy way is to place a cardboard tube on the edge and roll the paper off the acrylic and onto the tube. You won't need to clean the surface. Quickly place the acrylic next to the poster before any dirt can get between them. With the acrylic in place you can remove the front paper.

You are now ready to install your braquettes. We prefer the clear ones because they are less obtrusive. They are also available in black and stainless steel. There are two main parts to the braquettes that are alike except one has a hanging provision on the back. Be sure you place the one with the hanger on top. If the braquettes will not fit on the foam core, acrylic, and poster, then merely pinch the foam core with a pair of pliers. If this is necessary, protect the front of the acrylic with a soft cloth. Now that they are on, pull the nylon string taut to extend the tension spring. Close the lock lever and tuck in the extra string but do not cut it off (you may need it for a different-size picture in the future).

You will be very pleased with this handsome and inexpensive way to frame a poster or print.

This champion football team gets special treatment. It is floating between 2 pieces of glass. A small mat in the team color and a brass frame add the finishing touch. For a special feature, have a plate engraved with details and mounted on the mat.

sports events

We all have a drawer or a box with mementos collected over the years—team pictures, class pictures, awards, and such— and we really do plan to get them all framed some day! But how do you do this without resorting to that standard black frame?

An undefeated football season prompted this special treatment at our house, and the reaction was so popular that we have continued to use it for many things. Its simplicity and originality go well with any decor or in a grouping. Win or lose, someone will feel very special with this finished project.

The ever-popular glass mat (we love it for so many occasions) was the starting point for this (see page 129). The team colors were used around the picture and just inside the simple

brass frame. Only $1/8''$ is used in both instances. For an extra-special touch a small brass plaque was engraved with the occasion and also mounted on the same-color mat. The glass mat is about $1^1/2''$.

Another nice award to frame is a banner won in competitions. The sailing banner from the yacht club was a favorite project for our teen-age son's room. The banner was put on white mat with linen tape, and a double mat of gray and navy surrounded it. The shiny red metal frame pulled this sporty-looking item together.

Whether it's a simple school picture or a very important award, you can plan an endless variety of interesting and fun ways to frame it. There are no set guidelines. Let your imagination be your guide!

stained glass

We saw it from across the room at an antique show and knew that we had to have it—a beautiful 20''×24'' antique stained-glass window.

We also knew that our stained-glass window had to have a very special frame. We wanted one that would not detract in any way from the beauty of the glass; we wanted it to look finished from both sides; and we wanted to preserve the authentic antique look. And when framing an art piece as heavy and fragile as this stained-glass window, one must also think in terms of strength.

As shown in the illustration, we chose to make our frame very wide and deep. So as not to have a backing, and because there was no lip and liner on the wood we used, we supported the window by attaching quarter round to all the inside edges of the frame on either side of the stained glass.

Raw maple was the wood we used—you could also use less-expensive preshaped pine. The wood needs to be deep enough to allow room for the glass and two pieces of ½'' quarter round. The glass in these windows was all hand-cut, and it is not unusual for one side to be fractionally larger than its counterpart.

We purchased two pieces, 4''×4''×24'', for about $10, and ½''×8' of quarter round. After measuring the appropriate width and length we used a table saw to cut the frame to four pieces, 1⁷/₈''×2¼''×2''.

After the wood was sawed we proceeded to sand the maple with a heavy grade of sandpaper, moving to a lighter grade as the roughness was sanded down. We cut the wood for the largest size. We also added ¹/₁₆'' all around to allow for expansion or contraction in the glass or frame due to the changing environment.

Use a miter box and saw to miter your corners. Sand any rough edges that the miters may have caused. Now you are ready to join the maple.

With one length and one width in the vise, glue the mitered corners together. For extra strength, and in keeping with the theme of the antique glass, we used wooden dowels instead of nails. We drilled two holes on one side of the maple and one hole on the other. Using a ¼'' drill bit, we drilled

The stained glass window (shown in color on back cover) is framed so that both sides appear to be the right side and it can be viewed from either side. Dowels are used instead of nails to give the stained glass window the special treatment it deserves.

2¼" into the wood. We cut ¼" dowels to a length of 2¼" and sharpened the end to a point with a utility knife. This helped when hammering the dowel into the maple. The hammering leaves the dowel slightly beaten up, so we left a bit sticking out and sanded it down smooth and flush with the frame. Do all the corners in the same way.

Before the final fitting, the oil or stain must be applied. We used a high-quality tung oil to bring out the rich wood grains. Rub the oil on with a clean rag, applying two or three coats. Since the quarter round is pine, you will need to experiment with stains to achieve the same color as the natural frame. After the stain dried we applied a few coats of oil on the quarter round. It soaks up more oil than the maple, so we had to apply four to five coats.

Now take the quarter round and miter it to fit the inside of the maple frame. You will need a total of eight pieces, as you will be lining both sides of the glass with it, so the frame can be viewed from either side. Set the quarter round back about ⅛" from the front of the frame along one edge, and nail it so the nails won't be visible, by angling them down through the

quarter
round 1/2"

stained glass

quarter
round 1/2"

Cross section

159

quarter round into the frame. Predrill these holes for ease in nailing and to prevent any damage to the frame. Use a bit that is just $1/32$nd smaller than the nail. Repeat this step along the other three sides and insert the frame.

Lay the frame face down on the table. Very carefully place the glass window on the quarter round that is attached to the maple frame.

Predrill holes in the four back pieces of quarter round, lay the sticks on the glass, and nail as you did in front. These nails will again be angled down through the quarter round and into the frame, but of course you are nailing on the arched side of the quarter round this time. Since the nailholes will show from the back, and the frame will be viewed from both sides, you can mix some of the stain with plastic wood or spackling compound and fill in the holes.

Put some brass screw eyes on top of the frame, use a brass chain or strong-gauge opaque fishing wire, and hang from decorative hooks in the ceiling. We hung ours in front of the closed side of our sliding glass door. When the sun shines through that glass, it is truly magnificent. It was one of our favorite and most enjoyable projects.

unusual frames

In our house anything that stands still can end up as a picture frame. If you look around and use your imagination there are countless things that can be used for a frame. Such was the case when a favorite aunt and uncle gave us an antique hat block. The beautiful wood and the shape were too good to pass up. A linen background and a small brass horn transformed the block into a shadow-box frame. Again the basic skills you have learned, such as cutting a mat and covering a mat, can be put to use here.

Simply cut a piece of mat board to fit into the back of the hat block. Spray glue the fabric on the mat board. Attach the horn with brass wire. Then attach it to the frame with brads. Don't use glass.

The finished object in our house is a conversation piece, an antique to be enjoyed, and, of course, a lovely wall decoration.

"updated" frames

In the fashion world we keep our clothes in step with the times by adding the right accessories. The same can be true of our frames. Old frames (not antique ones—those we *want* to look old) can lose their tacky look by the addition of some fresh paint and a pretty fabric mat or liner. Perhaps you were a craft enthusiast and have some craft frames around. They work well on photos and decrease the cost when you do a whole gallery or bookcase at one time.

Sometimes, to save money, a picture is given a simple frame. Later this frame can be used as a liner, and an additional frame can be added. Make the new frame to fit the outside dimension of the old frame. Brads can be used to fit it up. If the old frame is in bad shape you can cover it with fabric and use it as a fabric liner.

If the frame is too outdated or in very bad shape, simply sand it down and cover the entire thing with fabric. If you have ever priced fabric frames you will really enjoy making your own.

DISASSEMBLING A FRAME

Often an old frame can be used on another picture. You may find some old frames at a garage sale or antique shop, or you may change the frame on a picture and save the old one. If you are going to cut down the old frame you must first disassemble it.

Great care should be taken in breaking down a frame so it can be used again. You will be chopping it down to a smaller size, and you do not want to ruin the finish of the frame. Therefore, when breaking the frame always remember to break the corners downward instead of upward. This will protect the top of the finish. If the corners cannot be broken with a simple breaking with both hands, a hard thrust is in order. Take the frame with both hands and hit the edge of a table with the back of a corner. Do all four corners this way. After the joint has been broken, each corner must be pried apart. This can be done with manual strength or with a pair of pliers

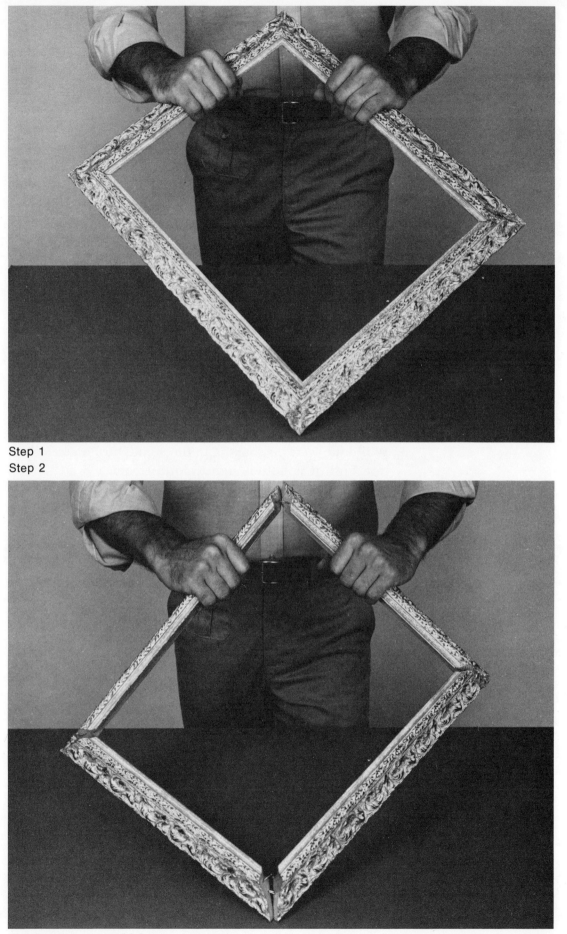

Step 1
Step 2

Breaking apart an old frame

and a screwdriver. After the corners have been completely disassembled, hammer the points of the nails and pull them out by the heads.

If you have access to a large vise, you can utilize it to take the frame apart. Lay a corner in the vise so one strip fits snugly in the vise and the other strip is just outside the brace. When you unscrew the vise on the side that does not hold the moulding snugly, it will break the joint. Do this to all four corners.

Before you saw the frame down, be certain that all the nails have been removed from the corners.

REMOVING A DENT IN THE MOULDING

If your frame is dented, try the following technique:

1. Take a straight pin and make tiny holes in the frame where the dent is. This is done so that the water in step 2 can penetrate the wood better.
2. Moisten the dent of the frame with several drops of water.
3. While the water is soaking in the wood, turn on a clothes iron until it is hot enough to form steam.
4. Moisten a paper towel and the wood where the dent is. Place the moistened paper towel over the wood (the towel should be folded once).
5. Place the tip of the hot iron on the paper towel very lightly—just enough, in fact, to cause steam to rise from the touch. This also causes the water in and on the wood to steam and will eventually cause the wood to swell back to its original structure. Repeat steps 2 through 5 until the dent no longer exists.

vogue prints
with metal frames

Art Deco prints that have been around for many years can be combined with almost any decor. This, in addition to their availability and low cost, make them especially attractive as a form of house decor. These pictures can be mounted on a black mat and framed using single off-white beveled mat and do-it-yourself metal frames.

In this project, follow the directions for mounting a print, employing black mat board instead of a mounting board. Spray glue only the back of the print, as some of the black mat will show. Bevel cut the off-white mat so that ¼″ of black shows all the way around the print. The metal frames come with easy instructions. You can use nonglare glass. The final results are sensational and will make people think you have put a great deal of time and money into the project.

Who would believe that these are only $1.00 prints? They are mounted on black mat board with ⅛″ showing on all four sides. Chrome frames and 2″ off-white mats add the final touch for a classy look that belies the cost.

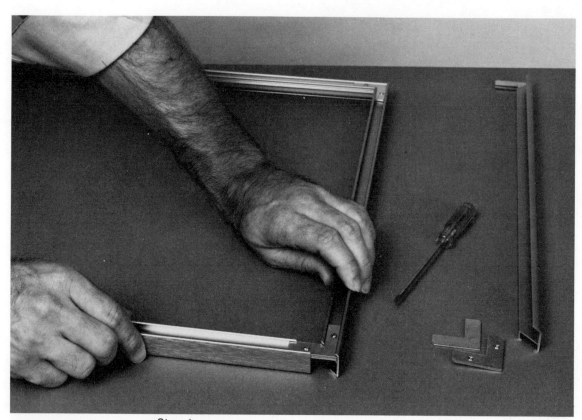

Step 1

Step 2

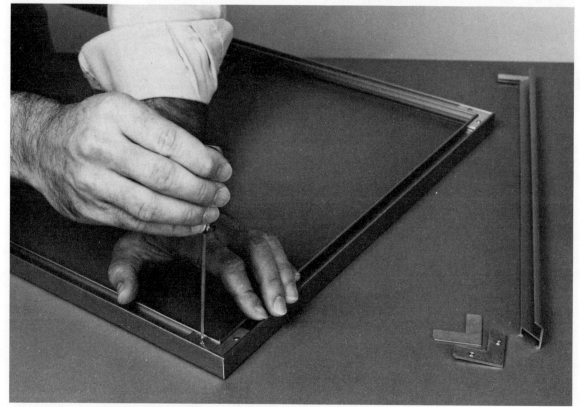

Joining an aluminum frame

166

wedding pictures

A wedding day is a very special one, and your pictures of it deserve special treatment. This is when you should use lovely silk mats and gold-leaf frames. Whether it is a formal wedding portrait or a candid shot, everyone enjoys a memento of the occasion. What a nice gift to give the bride and groom—a framed picture.

In our picture an ivory silk mat is bordered by a pale blue silk liner. They are both on top of the glass, so nonglare glass can be used. A gold-leaf frame with simple lines is used so as not to compete with the bride and groom.

You can also pick a series of candids from the reception and do a small grouping. You can use a single frame and a mat with three or four openings can be covered with fabric. Our chapter on mat cutting and covering leads you through the steps to complete this project.

Another nice memento to frame is the wedding invitation. You can use fabric or paper mats. An ivory mat with a small gold liner is nice, and again, the gold-leaf frames are favorites.

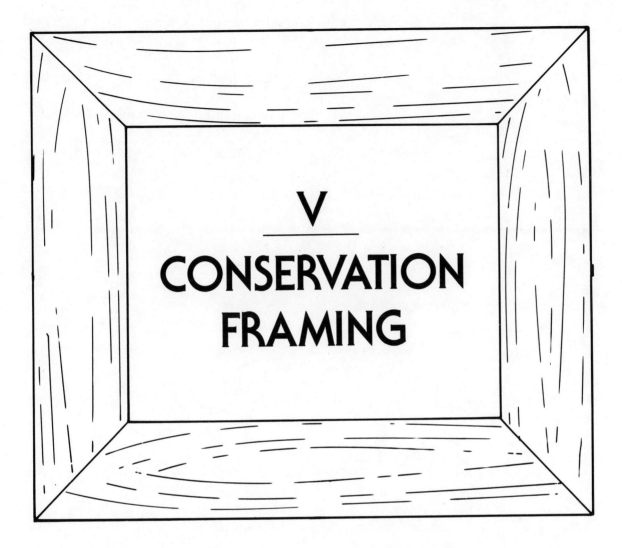

V

CONSERVATION FRAMING

CONSERVATION FRAMING IS an art in itself. The purpose of this chapter is not to provide instruction, but to educate serious art collectors in the proper methods of conservation framing, so that they can be certain their own works are properly done.

fine artwork on paper or parchment

FINE ARTWORK INCLUDES watercolors, pastels, etchings, limited editions, lithographs, sentimentally valuable pictures, pictures bought for investment and possible resale, and documents, certificates, and diplomas.

There are certain steps that must be followed when handling fine artwork:

1. Always wash hands thoroughly before handling.
2. Lift carefully, using two hands and the two top corners.
3. When putting artwork in storage, it should first be matted with museum or rag board front and back, using an acid-free hinge.
4. When measuring a picture for a frame or mat, avoid placing the ruler directly over the front of the picture; rather, measure from the outside edge of the picture. If it is necessary to measure directly over the picture, allow a space of air as a safety measure.
5. Never use pressure-sensitive tape such as masking tape, any kind of glue, brown gummed tape, spray glue, or a heat-sealing method. Use only the materials described later.
6. When transporting fine artwork unframed, sandwich the matted picture between two stiff boards (an exception is pastels; they require special attention). Lay the pastels, charcoals, pencil drawings, etc. in a box so the surface is never touched. These are not shipping instructions, merely local transportation instructions (from store to car to home, etc.). Leave the shipping to the experts, as that is an art in itself.
7. When storing unframed artwork, you can sandwich the matted piece between two pieces of four-ply rag board and seal the edges all the way around with linen tape. Store the artwork flat. Cut the museum board about 1″ larger than the picture all the way around for an extra measure of caution (the exception, of course, is the pastel; you can tape the outermost edge of the matted

pastel to the bottom of the box so it won't shift around; be sure the box is stable, and store flat).

MEASURING

1. When measuring a piece of artwork, be sure that the ruler does not touch the artwork. If it is necessary to measure directly over the picture, then allow a space of air between artwork and ruler.
2. Always measure to leave about ¼″ between the picture and the wood part of the frame. If the picture is framed touching the wood, the acid from the wood will cause the picture to be stained brown. If a mat is not to be employed here, the entire interior of the frame should be lined with rag board.

MOUNTING

1. Again, 100% rag board will be used as a backing board to go directly against the back of the picture.
2. The backing board is to be cut to the same outside dimensions as the mat.

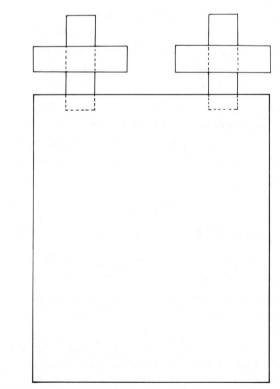

Recommended hinging procedure for fine art on paper.

3. When installing the picture on the rag board, a fine-quality hinge should be used. There is only one type. The materials used are a starch paste and a pH-neutral paper.
4. There are two hinging procedures most commonly used: the tab hinge, for smaller pictures (less than $11'' \times 14''$); and the T hinge, for any picture larger than $11'' \times 14''$. Two hinges should be applied at the top of the picture, *near* (not at) the corners.

MATTING

1. We highly recommend matting the picture. Use 100% rag board. This is a high-quality board available in four-ply or two-ply. We recommend using the four-ply in the conservation frame. Rag board is made up of high-quality cotton fibers. This is a nonacidic board and will conserve your valued piece of art for many decades to come. Although rag board is a high quality material, it should be tested for a pH rating. This can be done with an archivist's pen.
2. A beveled mat is much more desirable when a single mat is employed. (See instructions for cutting a beveled mat).
3. There are colored all-rag boards on the market that have been proven safe. Strathmore and Alpha rag are two of these.
4. If you desire color, there are alternatives (see OPTIONS AND VARIATIONS IN MATTING, following).
5. If the artwork is not to be matted, narrow strips of four-ply rag board must be glued *on the glass* with white glue. This four-ply rag will separate glass from picture.

OPTIONS AND VARIATIONS IN MATTING

The design of a conservation-framed object can be very limited; however, we have a few ideas that can add color and imagination to fine art on paper or parchment and still retain the high quality of the conservation frame.

1. Use two pieces of rag board (four-ply) in a double matting effect. You will find that this adds an extra dimension. We recommend using a bevel on both cuts. For

example, if the mat border on the top mat is 3″– 3″–
3″–3½″, the bottom mat will be 3¼″–3¼″–3¼″–3¾″.

2. Also you can use architectural tape in a French matting effect as mentioned in the section in "Variations on a Mat."

3. Curved corners can also be utilized (these are also mentioned in the matting section). These can be used with a straight cut only.

4. Of course you can use color. Cut any regular mat board to the desired dimensions, then cover it with a fabric (a color of your choice). Now glue the covered mat to the *top* of the glass; in this way the acid in the colored fabric will not affect the valued artwork at all. Regular mat board should not be glued to the front of the glass, as the mat board will deteriorate much faster than the fabric mat on glass. Thin fabrics and white fabrics should be avoided.

5. Remember that a four-ply rag board should still be utilized between the glass and the picture.

6. On the framed artwork with the fabric mat on top of the glass, this is how the frame should be constructed (from front to back): frame, fabric mat glued to glass, glass, four-ply rag mat, artwork hinged to the four-ply rag board, cardboard sealed with gummed brown tape, and the dust cover.

Above: Popular wildlife artist John P. Cowan has signed and numbered this print, so conservation framing is employed here. Again, the mats are on top of the glass so you can design it to suit your taste. Left: Conservation framing is used to protect this antique map. All mats are on top of the glass and ragboard is used next to the map.

points to remember
when choosing the glass
in conservation framing

1. For a conservation-frame job, acrylic should be chosen. It is manufactured by Rohm, Haas (under the name Plexiglas) and by Dupont (under the name Lucite).
2. Acrylic is a better thermal insulator than glass. This means that acrylic reacts much slower to a temperature change than glass; thus condensation is not as likely to occur with acrylic. Also, with acrylic the strain of rapid contraction and expansion is greatly reduced for the artwork.
3. Acrylic is a must when shipping a picture, as its strength is unmatched by that of any glass. If a picture has been framed with regular glass and should be accidentally dropped, the chances that your valuable work of art will be damaged are greatly increased.
4. Acrylic has much better clarity than window glass—that is, the colors of a picture will be truer (less distorted).
5. Acrylic is lighter than regular glass or nonglare.
6. Acrylic is available with an ultraviolet filter. This means that if your picture is exposed to sunlight or fluorescent lighting, the ultraviolet rays will be greatly reduced.
7. The popularity of nonglare glass forces us to make a statement about its value. Nonglare glass is most functional when used directly against a picture; however, in a conservation frame this is not feasible. Using nonglare glass with one mat is barely passable, but with two mats it should *never* be used. Personally we would never use it in a conservation frame.
8. Always remember that light fades and weakens the cellular structure of paper. A low level of light adds tremendously to the longevity of your art.

different media on parchment or paper

PARCHMENT

1. Parchment is traditionally used for documents and certificates.
2. Parchment is animal skin—sheep, goat, calf, etc.
3. Due to extra processing costs for animal skin, use of parchment is becoming rare for documents. Parchment in good condition should never be reinforced or mounted. The color of parchment is very pleasing to the eye, but if parchment is mounted with a permanent glue, it can assume an ugly, yellowish-brown color (because of the opacity of the parchment). Thus off-white or white four-ply rag board should be used directly behind the parchment.

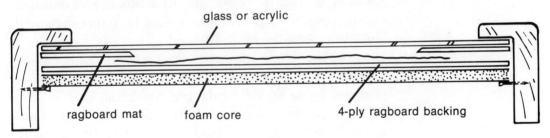

glass or acrylic

ragboard mat   foam core   4-ply ragboard backing

Cross section

4. If parchment is stored between two pieces of rag board, the parchment will stay reasonably flat. If the parchment is left in a cylindrical container until framed, it will be cylindrical.
5. If the parchment is given to you in a special fold-out container, check the container for acidity (for example, over a period of time, school colors in ribbons or tassels will fade the parchment).
6. Never allow the parchment to get wet, as the ink may run, and the skin would be turned to gelatin. Also, there would be more chance of mold growth.
7. If you own a valuable or antique diploma on parchment

and it has been stored folded for many years, don't attempt to open it, as the parchment may break in your hands. Consult a conservator.

8. There are many imitation parchments on the market. There are two ways to determine real parchment: (1) Hold the certificate up to the light; if the velnous structure is inconsistent, the certificate is real parchment. (2) Caress the certificate between your fingers; if it feels velvety, it is parchment.

PASTELS

1. Never apply a spray fixative to a pastel. A pastel's character is in the flatness in texture; if a fixative is used on a pastel, it will lose the texture.
2. Avoid the slightest jolt as this will cause the pastel to loosen and eventually fall off the paper. Frame as soon as possible.
3. Be sure the pastel is framed properly the first time; excess handling should be avoided.
4. Never allow the surface of the pastel to be touched by anything.
5. A pastel should be stored flat in a box before framing.
6. Avoid dampness. Collectors should be concerned with humidity curtailment.
7. Inspect the front of pastels periodically for fungus growth. If the fungus is observed quickly enough, most of it can be removed. Consult a conservator.
8. Remove pastels from the room when it is to be fumigated for bugs.

WATERCOLORS

1. Watercolors are extremely susceptible to fading so seriously consider the ultraviolet-filter acrylic. We recommend the Rohm & Haas Plexiglas No. UF-3.
2. Watercolors are most enhanced by a mat.

stretched canvas

1. Felt should be employed on the lip of the frame or liner. Over time a canvas will expand and contract in a frame. If there is friction it will actually cause the paint on the edges of the canvas to be scraped off.

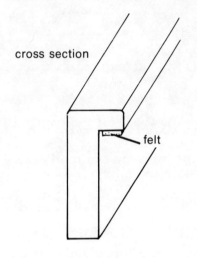

cross section

felt

2. When restretching a canvas, never trim off excess canvas in the back. Later the canvas may have to be restretched, and it should remain intact for this purpose.
3. If you have a stretched canvas that is defenseless to an occasional curious touch or an accidental elbow, we suggest moving it, or installing acrylic in the frame. This acrylic should be separated from the canvas by a double layer of four-ply rag board.
4. Acrylics on canvas are much less susceptible than oils on canvas to fading due to ultraviolet rays from the sun or fluorescent lighting.
5. When fitting a canvas, *use thin nails when you put the canvas in the frame;* the canvas must be able to move, and thin, bent-over nails will allow this movement.
6. When finishing off the fitted canvas, be sure to use a stiff board attached to the back of the frame extending across the back of the canvas, as this will protect the canvas from being pierced and will keep bugs out. If it is not feasible to use cardboard on the back, then double up on the dust cover.

*A real treasure—President Andrew Jackson signed
this document. To ensure that no further damage
occurs to this document, double-beveled rag board
is used and an ultra-violet filtered acrylic is chosen
instead of glass.*

"don'ts" in conservation framing

1. Never cut or fold artwork done on paper or parchment, as this will destroy its aesthetic value. Evidence of authenticity could be destroyed, thus destroying the resale value.

2. A fine work of art on paper or parchment should never be permanently mounted but can be reinforced or lined by a conservator in the case of a weakened or damaged document. Spray glue, rubber cement, white glue, epoxy, silicone, or any other type of permanent glue will cause the resale value to drop to *zero*. Use the prescribed hinges discussed in the section on conservation framing and mounting.

3. Glass should never touch the picture.

4. Leave all restorations to your local conservator. One can be located through your nearest fine arts museum.

5. Never nail through a stretcher strip when fitting a canvas.

6. Cardboard should not be used directly behind a fine work of art. Use only four-ply rag board.

7. Acidic mat board should not be used next to the picture. Again, use only four-ply rag board as a mat next to the picture.

factors dangerous to artwork

AIR POLLUTION

There are chemicals in the air (especially in city areas, where there are a lot of cars and manufacturing plants) that will destroy fine artwork on paper or parchment. These chemicals are sulphur dioxide, sulfuric acid, nitrous oxide, etc.

PREVENTIVE MEASURES:
1. Be absolutely sure that the dust cover is intact on the back of the frame. If the dust cover is torn, have it repaired immediately.

INSECTS

Insect destroyers of paper and parchment are silverfish, termites, cockroaches, and woodworms.

PREVENTIVE MEASURES:
1. Have your home exterminated at least twice a year. Discuss the types of insects you see crawling around your home. Also, you might inquire about different chemicals in an effort to seek out the ones that will be just as effective and less harmful to your works of art.
2. Check the back of the framed picture for a hole or tear in the dust cover, as it must remain sealed. If there is a tear in the dust cover, then the picture is defenseless against those little creatures. If the dust cover is torn, be sure to check the contents of the frame, as one of those little guys may have entered through the back door.

LIGHT

1. All light fades works of art on paper or parchment. This is especially true of sunlight and fluorescent light; these

contain an ultraviolet radiation, which is extremely harmful. Light also breaks down the cellulose chain in paper—that is, weakens the paper structure.

1. Avoid placing pictures in direct sunlight in a room. If there are no alternatives try rotating picture placement. This can be done from room to room or in the same room. This will not allow any one picture to be exposed to sunlight for a great length of time.
2. Curtains or louvered blinds may be utilized to cut off strong sunlight, especially during peak sunshine hours.
3. As for fluorescent lighting, there are special sleeves that can be placed around fluorescent bulbs that will filter out those damaging ultraviolet rays. You can also buy acrylic sheeting, which can be placed in front of the picture (instead of using glass with an ultraviolet filter manufactured in the acrylic). There are two companies that manufacture this item: Rohm & Haas (Plexiglas) and Du Pont (Lucite). I am familiar with the Rohm & Haas acrylic and have been very satisfied with its performance.

HUMIDITY

Among the factors dangerous to fine artwork, humidity has to be ranked at the top of the list. Excessive humidity promotes fungus (mildew and mold) that shows up on the picture in brown spots called *foxing*. The fungus gets its nourishment from the paper, thus weakening it and eventually deteriorating it.

There are, of course, preventive measures you can take. Of course, some will be more practical for you than others; but the life of your artwork depends on prevention.

PREVENTIVE MEASURES:
1. Use a dehumidifier to keep the humidity below 65%.
2. Do not store fine artwork in attics or cellars. Do not hang fine artwork in bathrooms, where it would be exposed to constant steam and heat.
3. Clean frames and areas surrounding it regularly as dust contains airborne mold spores.
4. Never frame the picture directly against the glass. If mold gets on the picture it would stick to the glass, and then you would have a double problem.

5. Circulation of art in front and back of the frame will lessen the chance of fungus growth. Attach a piece of wood, cork, or even two screw eyes on the bottom back corners of the frame. This will allow the air to circulate freely on both sides of the picture. Air conditioning helps circulate air.
6. Don't leave pictures in a closed house (for example, a summer home) for long periods of time without fresh air.
7. Don't hang pictures near a heat source, as the drastic temperature change will be a strain on the paper or parchment.
8. Acrylic can be used instead of glass. Acrylic is a thermal insulator and reacts much slower than glass to temperature change.

If you notice there is fungus on a picture, there is a preventive measure you can take. Unframe and let circulating air dry the picture.

If your picture has the brown spots called foxing, it would be worthwhile to contact a conservator. Art conservators have many years of experience and study concerning such problems. If you don't know of one, contact your local fine-arts museum for the name of a conservator.

additional points to remember

1. If you own a picture that is showing signs of spotting and streaking (usually brown in color), the picture must be immediately removed and the contents examined, as there may be cardboard where there should be rag board.
2. The occurrence of static electricity cannot be permanently eliminated from acrylic; however, static electricity can be temporarily reduced with an antistatic cleaning solution.
3. Remember, fungi (mold and mildew) thrive on three basic ingredients: dampness, darkness, and warmth.
4. Any information pertinent to the artwork that has been framed should be placed in a white envelope and attached to the back of the frame. In this manner any information about the artwork will be readily accessible. Information should also be available as to the exact contents of the framed picture and mounting procedures.
5. After a picture has been framed, mark the date on the back of dust cover, as the picture should be examined at least once every ten years.

select bibliography

Dollof, Francis W., & Perkinson, Roy L. *How to Care for Works of Art on Paper*. Boston: Museum of Fine Arts, 1971.

Fall, Frieda Kay. *Art Objects: Their Care and Preservation*. California: Laurence McGilvery, 1971.

Plenderleith, H. J., and Werner, A. E. A. *The Conservation of Antiquities and Works of Art*. London/New York: Oxford University Press, 1962.

INDEX

Heinz Kugler

ABOUT THE AUTHORS

A fifth-generation Texan and a native Houstonian, Sherwood McCall has been a professional picture framer since 1967. His wife Connie came to Houston in 1961. She is a graduate of Centenary College for Women and has a background in the arts and crafts field.

They have done picture framing demonstrations for the X-acto Co., and their projects have appeared in Better Homes and Gardens' *Christmas Ideas* (1976) and the *Better Homes and Gardens Treasury of Christmas*.

The McCalls are very involved in family activities, including Scouts, Little League, and the Presbyterian Church, where Sherwood is an ordained deacon. This is their first book.